Brain Unchained

Shining a torch on depression and lighting the way to emotional awareness in teenagers and young adults.

Kay Reeve

Disclaimer

This book is designed to provide information and motivation to our readers. It is sold with the understanding that the author and publisher are not engaged to render any type of psychological, legal, or any other kind of professional advice. The content is the sole expression and opinion of its author. Neither the publisher nor the individual author(s) shall be liable for any physical, psychological, emotional, financial, or commercial damages, including, but not limited to, special, incidental, consequential or other damages. Our views and rights are the same: You are responsible for your own choices, actions, and results.

The content of the book is solely written by the author.

DVG STAR Publishing are not liable for the content of the book.

Published by DVG STAR PUBLISHING

www.dvgstar.com

email us at info@dvgstar.com

ISBN: 1-912547-54-6
ISBN-13: 978-1-912547-54-8

DEDICATION

To my son Matthew, who has been the biggest inspiration for my book. He has been the toughest challenge of my life yet provides some of the most rewarding moments when we get life right.

Thank you to my daughter Heidi for her many years of patience and loving towards her younger brother. She has been a rock and a big softie in one, despite also having her own challenges to face, growing up, finding work and starting her own family.

Hugs to my three beautiful Grandchildren, Dylan, Holly and Lily. Dylan, in his first year alone, helped prove my theories in this book to be helpful. No matter how young or how simple your problems may be, a bad day is still a bad day, and the lessons in this book can help parents to understand their children better.

Most importantly, a very big thank you to my Husband Denis, who has stood by my side, providing for us all. He had supported and backed me through some of the most challenging decisions of my life when others around me had different opinions. These decisions included me giving up work to home educate our children, putting more pressure on him to work long hours. He has always been my rock, keeping me strong while I always ensured that our family came first above everything else.

I love you all so much.

Kay Reeve

FOREWORD

The mind is a complex machine.

Professionally, I understand Adolescent Mental Health and have many explanations as to why this machine might break down. As a Mum, with a son who faces his own mental health challenges, it's a totally different ballgame! I have sometimes felt powerless in not knowing how best to support him; probably because my own emotions tend to cloud my judgement.

I have often felt lost and confused. Until now.

Brain Unchained has given me the tools I need to feel more confident in my own parenting approach. Not only that, but using "The Mood Mentor Model", I have another tool in my toolbox that will better equip me in supporting other children in my care.

Teenagers don't like being told what to do, especially by their own parents! So equipping them with a system that helps them understand their own minds and offers solutions to dealing with life's challenges, gives them back the control they need to move forward with more confidence.

Whilst there may indeed be "light at the end of the tunnel" - if you don't know how that tunnel is laid out or indeed how long it is - then these words offer very little reassurance. Kay's simple but mindful system is the blueprint in finding that light, faster and more easily.

Cai Graham: Mum, Bestselling Author of The TEEN Toolbox™, Podcaster and International Speaker.

CONTENTS

USING THIS BOOK...1

INTRODUCTION 3

WHAT IS THE MOOD MENTOR MODEL? 8

CHAPTER 1: EMOTIONAL AWARENESS.....................13

    C.I.O. MODEL 14

    MEET YOURSELF - THE EXPERT...........................15

    MIND MAP – GET EVERYTHING OUT............................19

    YOUR STARTING POINT 26

    RECOGNISING WHEN YOU ARE LOST 30

    HITTING ROCK BOTTOM 36

STEP 1: CORE EMOTIONS 46

    YOUR EMOTIONAL CYCLE 50

    YELLOW – HAPPY..55

    SAD – BLUE 59

    ANGRY – RED 63

    BLACK – DEPRESSED...67

    POSITIVES VS NEGATIVES....................................71

STEP 2: CHANGE 79

    INNER CHANGE...91

    OUTER CHANGE 99

CHAPTER 2: OPTIONS 111

    5 STEP MODEL FOR H.E.L.P.S. 114

    HEALTH 115

    EMOTIONAL 130

    LOGICAL 144

    PHYSICAL 155

    SOCIAL 170

CHAPTER 3: ROOT CAUSE 190

    5 STEP MODEL FOR F.L.I.T.E. 191

    FINANCE 192

    LINKS 199

    INFORMATION 207

    TIME 218

    ENERGY 228

BRAIN UNCHAINED SUMMARY 237

EMPATHY – PAYING IT FORWARD 239

KAY AND HER SON MATTHEW 240

AUTHOR AND TEDx SPEAKER 242

ACKNOWLEDGEMENTS 244

TESTIMONIAL 245

USING THIS BOOK

Information will be in standard text like this.

Exercises will be clearly headed as EXERCISES, or there will be lined spaces to write in throughout the book with questions to help you think about your life more clearly.

There will be personal and conversational messages from me throughout the book. I want you to think of it as sitting across the table from me, and having a chit-chat about life:

"These chats and messages will be in a script like this"

Treat the book like an exercise book and make notes in pencil (or pen).

If you really don't want to write in the book, you can make notes and answer questions in a separate notebook, so you can check back later and see the progress you are making.

Parent toolbox has been boxed in grey for parents to work alongside their teens.

Key points from each chapter are indicated in bold.

"Sometimes you just need a break in a beautiful place alone, to figure everything out."

Coco Chanel

INTRODUCTION

Staying calm in stressful situations is not an easy state to achieve.

Imagine a paramedic who remains calm at the scene of a car crash while everyone else panics. This is because he is both trained and equipped to deal with the situation at hand.

A bystander who witnesses an accident may feel panic, hopelessness or even fear. This panic doesn't stop when the incident is over, creating flashbacks and memories that still haunt you after the event.

Let's take a quick check-in at the scene...

- What about the person who was driving the car? How does he feel?
- What about any passengers or witnesses?
- What about the owner of the fence that was broken?

Try and think about how many different emotions control every one of these people immediately after the accident. They are all at the same accident, yet every one of them is feeling a different emotion.

Are each of them in control of their emotions?

Try and put yourself in each of their shoes. Think about whether you would be in control of your emotions, or would your emotions take control of you.

So how does the paramedic manage to stay calm? How does he stay in control of his emotions in all this chaos?

- This book will teach you to understand why your emotions take the path they do.
- Recognise changes in your emotions.
- When life takes the rough road, learn to find your own way back-on-track.

This book uses a combination of *constant personal analysis* and *positive mind-set*.

That may sound a bit grown-up and corporate, but every journey starts with the first steps. This book is about *your first steps, which include* overcoming depression, stress, or anxiety. Let me re-phrase that for you...

This book helps you become aware of your own feelings and emotions in a constructive way that will help you for life.

- It trains you to recognise and analyse your own feelings, including good emotions.
- It helps you learn to recognise unhelpful feelings and turn them around.
- You will learn about *emotional toolsets* for *creating change.*

*Be **empowered** to handle challenges and make positive changes!*

You may find some areas in this book will reinforce *your* existing methods of handling stressful situations, while other areas could help your moods improve or create calm where there was chaos. You may even see an improvement in the people around you, as you create the ripple effect of happiness.

With time, practice and consistency, you will learn to trust your feelings and intuition. You will learn the importance of connecting with others as the authority, or go-to persons, in times of emotional crisis.

Throughout the book, you will spend time thinking about your own experiences and what causes you stress. You will learn to relate those thoughts to why or how it may be driving your emotional challenges.

You will also learn the importance of working through the process and never giving up.

A young lady I know, said last year that she was going to cancel her counselling sessions as they were making her feel worse.

I helped her realise that therapy is like sorting out your cupboards. If you only take out a couple of items and put them back, it's tidier, but you didn't sort out the cupboard.

When you're truly halfway through, then everything is out on the floor, and it looks a mess, but that's when you get rid of the junk.

Items no one else wants to see can always be re-packed at the back of the cupboard or thrown away, but if you give up sorting a cupboard halfway through, then everything gets left out in a mess for everyone to see.

She did see the sessions through and was grateful for the inspiration.

As a young adult, you have some of the most exciting times ahead of you. You also have some of the most challenging times ahead, moving between childhood and adulthood, sorting a career and more.

It will, at times, feel like this big void that seems impossible to cross and gets scary in the middle. Just like the young lady above, be aware that the middle is often tough, but really important to get through, no matter how hard it is to keep going.

Throughout this book, you will learn about 'your own emotional cycle', and by using the Mood Mentor Model discover how emotions can hinder you, create stress, depression and anxiety, or how it can help you take control of your life, finding happiness and success.

When my son was nineteen years old, in the deepest darkest depression and couldn't connect with time or tell the day of the week, he was feeling suicidal once again. I had exhausted all options and needed a 'visual' way to teach him how to understand his own emotions one small step at a time. This is where the Mood Mentor Model began.

*"Science is organised knowledge –
Wisdom is organised life."*

Immanuel Kant 1724 – 1804
German philosopher of the mind

WHAT IS THE MOOD MENTOR MODEL?

The 'Mood Mentor' Model is a method I use to teach emotional intelligence. That's a way to understand your emotions better, and those of people around you.

The system is based around the use of colour to understand emotions. The colours are placed in the diagram, to represent the exact place they would be if you could see your own emotional cycle. The same pattern is reflected in your use of language, tone of voice, and body language.

Yellow

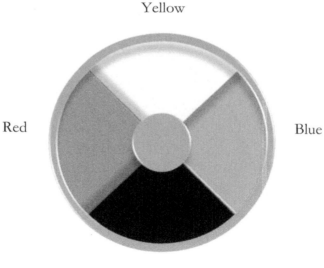

Red   Blue

Black

You will be surprised as you start to understand this diagram, that it's already the most fundamental part of who you are. This diagram is not something I simply made up and attached to; it's the pattern of emotions that already exist in everyone. It's *your* emotions made visible.

I saw this pattern in everyone's emotions globally, and in animals too. It's universal, no matter what age, religion, colour, sex, which football fan you are, or what latest designer handbag you carry. This is at the core of every human being. Now I can use it to teach you how to understand your emotions too.

I didn't invent the emotional cycle; it already exists just as pictured. It's understanding this cycle and making it a visual concept that is my speciality.

NO ONE has ever drawn the emotional cycle like this, until now. It has always been thought of as invisible. Many coaching models, charts and diagrams have been created to explain various behaviours and thought processes. Yet, they are all niche topics that start with one thing in mind, understanding emotions. This is the most basic lesson behind them all that has never been approached in this way before.

Now I can help you learn about your emotions in a whole new way, that can help you, not just now, but your entire life.

- **AWARENESS** - Imagine being on a journey, and not knowing you are walking in the wrong direction. Wouldn't you want to know, so you can start heading the 'right' way? Emotional Awareness will help you identify the signs that your emotions are taking you in the right or the wrong direction.

- **OPTIONS** - You only change between emotions because something changed, either negatively or positively. Recognising these changes to your emotions are essential to understanding how to stop yourself from going down the wrong path and make the right changes instead.

- **ROOT-CAUSE** - Each change that happens in life has a root cause. Learning these root causes gives you an understanding of where barriers block your journey and give you the keys to finding your way through these barriers, to discover success and true joy in life.

Each of these models can be used together, alone, or you can dip into a single point at any moment in life, to help you break through those emotional and real-life barriers that leave your brain feeling chained up.

This three-tier model is the secret to having your Brain Unchained and discovering the power of personal development.

"I lost myself trying to please everyone else. Now I'm losing everyone while I'm finding myself."

Buddha

CHAPTER 1: EMOTIONAL AWARENESS

Awareness is the first step to changing anything in your life.
The question is: How does 'your' self-awareness serve you?

. . . .

You have to be the student of your own mind, before you
can become the expert of your own mind.
unknown

. . . .

C.I.O. MODEL

C	Core-Emotions
I	Inner-Change
O	Outer-Change

Discovering Your Emotional Cycle

The C.I.O. Model will be explained throughout chapter one and builds a solid foundation for emotional resilience.

The concept of understanding your emotional cycle focuses on four Core Emotions, and what changes between your emotions. This encompasses a lot of dynamics such as inner thoughts, outer influences, positive and negative thinking, and helping you spot your strengths and weaknesses, so you have a great starting point called Emotional Awareness. You can then level-up in chapters two and three to develop Emotional Intelligence and problem-solving skills.

MEET YOURSELF - THE EXPERT

Whether you're a teenager, young adult, mature for your age, or never want to grow up; I'm here to help you understand more about yourself and improve on 'who you are', not change who you are. It is not intended to remove 'who you are' or make you a boring person. On the contrary, I want to hear that you've learned to find your true self and come alive.

I want you to realise just how much control you have over your own emotions, and how to drive them effectively—no more letting your emotions drive you.

YOU are the expert who knows yourself best.

In this book, I will teach you how to....
- leverage this concept
- that *you are your own expert.*
- You will learn how to listen to your own fears, anxieties and thoughts constructively.
- You will learn why you have these negative feelings, and how they are 'supposed' to help you.
- You will then learn to turn these negative emotions into something positive.

Not everyone has access to therapy right at that moment they need it. Some waiting lists can be months long, or some processes can take over a year. If you really need these, then stick with them. However, not everyone wants or needs therapy but could do with a little extra support. This book provides you with that support to help you learn how to ultimately be your own mentor.

You CAN Mentor yourself - and take control of your own life! Let me show you how...

Ideally you will mentor yourself through most of this book on your own. There could be that occasional time you need to have a real-life conversation with someone - to work through some issues, or maybe to help with some of the exercises set out for you. Think who that person may be that can help you. It could be a parent, teacher or even an elderly friend.

Make sure your helper is someone you trust, who already knows how to manage their own emotions, otherwise, they could give you the wrong advice, or make you feel worse about trying to help yourself.

Everyone says we should talk about depression and anxiety, and they are right to an extent, but it's more important that you learn to manage your own emotions effectively in the long term. Following this book will set you up for life rather than just working through a single problem. There will be times that it's good to talk, but we'll cover that as a subject in the book.

Suppose you have been subjected to sexual, emotional, or physical trauma and this book doesn't quite answer your concerns. In that case, I strongly suggest seeking more professional help to work over your specific barriers.

You will learn more in the chapter about
- why connecting with the 'right' people is essential,
- why it is vital to get professional help, and not expect a friend or family member to help with certain emotional issues.

The rest of the information in this book, will help you stay on track afterwards, reduce the likelihood of a relapse, and teach you to recognise and overcome relapses quickly, should they happen. Only *you* know the unique experiences that you have lived through. Some of your experiences would have had a positive benefit to your emotions such as a favourite song, a compliment from a teacher, or winning a trophy at your favourite sport. Other experiences possibly took something away from you emotionally, like bullying, exam stress or the loss of someone close.

This self-help book will assist you in searching through all your experiences to understand your own internal feelings.

Parent Toolbox

Alternatively, you may be the parent or mentor supporting a young person through this book. This will help you to support them in being their own expert. It is still them, who knows best, what's in their own mind. This book will help you support them through the process of learning about their emotions.

Helping your teenager to understand themselves is a long process of growth and can seem relentless at times but keep going. Just like that journey of a thousand miles, every single step forward is progress. Keep making small steps rather than looking at the whole journey. Recognise that just as adults face challenges daily, a teenager has the additional challenges of studying multiple topics, dealing with hormones, social anxiety in school or starting work, and the pressure of expectation from family and teachers. They don't always know what they want from life, yet trying to make life-changing decisions, knowing that soon they also need to take responsibility for their own finances and become independent. Phew, that's a LOT of pressure!

I'm sure if you think back, you felt the pressure of transitioning from teenager to adult life both physically and socially. The transition from education into further education or work, and the transition of all the social circles each time, with new friends, new teachers, new managers and colleagues. Leaving home and starting to pay your bills, fall in love and fall out of love. It all happens in a few short years and is a LOT to transition through while many of them also suffer Teenage Brain where brain activity slows during puberty.

What do you do when you don't know where to get the best advice?

If you feel that you are giving life everything you have, but there's something you are missing or can't quite put your finger on......

Start here!

Key Points

It is all very overwhelming for them, and for you as a parent wanting to keep them safe and help them grow. Rather than adding more pressure, try just being there for them. It is a journey of growth for you as a parent too, in supporting them through these difficult times. Never ever give up!

MIND MAP – GET EVERYTHING OUT

I've heard several names for this exercise. **Mind Map,** however, is the best term to search *online* for ideas on how to create your own mind map.

- *Ball Blasts*
- *Mind Maps*
- *Lists or Charts*
- *Doodles*
- *Scrap Booking*

I like the term **Ball Blast.** It has that *'Let it all out'* feeling to it and doesn't require any artistic input. Mind Map sounds a little corporate and organized. I'm betting your mind is not feeling corporate right now, but it also explains clearly about mapping out why you feel emotionally lost, and how to find your way again. As I know it as a **Mind Map**, I will refer to it as that throughout the book, but you can call it anything you wish.

It's important with a Mind Map that you let all the available information flow from your mind and put it onto paper, but also feel comfortable with adding more later. The more information you can put down, the better it will help. Shall we continue?

So why do I need to do a Mind Map?

Starting points are just as important in any journey as the destination. If you don't know where you are starting on a map, how can you give directions to a destination? Try it and see. This is
the reason you get mad, when people throw advice at you about growing up, and you say...

"You DON'T UNDERSTAND!"

Think of yourself, trying to give directions to somewhere, but the person travelling hasn't told you where they are starting, what type of transport they are using etc. How can you tell them which turnings to take and which routes are best, if you haven't *understood* their journey first? The same applies to your daily emotional journey and people giving you random advice. This could be parents, friends, teachers, a doctor, or a therapist. They can only help if you help them to help you by telling them where you are now. So why not get a head-start, or simply be strong and independent by working it out yourself with my help from the book below.

If you want to help yourself through life's challenges, even you will need to know where you are now, and where you want to go. Sometimes you will have to come back and check the map, find where you are again, and set a new course depending on changes that happen in life. Change is guaranteed as life never stays the same. This is why I say

....

Mastering Life is all about Mastering Change.
Kay Reeve

....

If you can't find your way on your own and need help from someone else, they need to know your starting point, so they can help you find the *right* directions.

Only when you can understand this concept of a starting point – where you are now - can you start taking steps on *your journey through life* in the right direction.

Are you steering your emotional journey right now?

Write down on a scale of 1–10 how much control you feel you have over your life and emotions at the moment.

Or are you simply free-wheeling and **hoping** you land somewhere nice?

How or what would you like to feel differently from now?

_____

What are you hoping to learn from this book?

_____

Make any other notes you would like to come back to later:

_____

_____

_____

_____

_____

_____

_____

_____

_____

_____

_____

EXERCISE 1:

MIND MAP WHERE ARE YOU?

I now want you to jump right into your first exercise and draw a map of your mind as it is now. I'll talk you through it, so it's not difficult, but will require some time to think. You can put it down and come back to is as often as you need, till you feel it is finished.

This mind map will help you see where you are right now, with challenges and emotions. This will be far more helpful than you think, so discipline yourself to get out the paper and pen, or some coloured pencils and crack on with it. It will also help you later, to see how much you've achieved when you look back at your progress.

Here's how to get the most out of a Mind Map:
1. Start by writing "Me" or "Your Name" in the centre of the paper and circle round it.
2. Around this, add *more* circles and label them for Family, Friends, School, Hobbies, etc.
3. Now look at each *new* label and break them down by adding circles outside. Around the family circle, for example, include family who are close to you. Do the same around friends.
4. Do the same around school or work, labelling subjects or tasks that are important.
5. Repeat this around each label. Don't think too deeply on any topic till the next round.
6. Now look at each of the outside circles and think of more detailed information you can add. For Family/Mum do you need to list Tasks, Pocket Money, or something else? Are you looking forward to a family holiday?
7. Repeat this for each other key label, by adding *details* to the outer circles.
8. Make another row of circles outside some of the topics if you need, but don't worry if you can't.

Great! Now the chart should look as neat or as scruffy as you chose, but what's more important is that you are looking at your own brain from the outside for a change.

The next few chapters will help you understand a little more about your core emotions; then we will re-visit your mind-map to see what your current emotional state is. Keep it somewhere safe till then.

If you're struggling with fitting everything on one mind map, try to expand on one of the subjects. Take a single label such as 'school' or 'hobby' and make that the centre of a whole new mind map. This helps if you have a lot more happening in one area of life, or there is something specific you feel like you need to work on. Come back here when you've done as much as you can. You can always add more to it over a few days.

So you've created a map of everything on your mind at the moment, good and bad. Let's start recording how the exercise has made you feel. Any answer is correct as only you will be looking back at it later.

Mood Mentor asks…

Now it's all on paper, how does it look?

Write your answer here

_____

_____

_____

How does it feel to see your thought from outside your head? Write it here

_____

_____

_____

When I did this exercise myself, just before leaving my work - to start my own business and write this book - I was juggling work, family, home, training, starting this book, making a website and still finding time for hobbies, holidays etc. Each of these became topics that were blasted into detailed subjects, problems, ideas, actions, barriers; then I looked at the paper afterwards and said to my husband…

"Wow! It's like my pen has just thrown up on the paper. No wonder my head was struggling so much!"

You see, our head gets so overloaded with daily life, that it's a way of standing back from yourself, looking at everything from a helicopter view while it stares back from that piece of paper - and you see yourself from a different angle.

So why can this book and the exercises help you? Think of it like this…

We are all good at advising our friends, but why not ourselves?

Now you can look at the mind map of yourself, your life, your problems and your strengths, with the same distance you would have when advising your friends. Imagine your parents keep giving you advice but getting it wrong. They know something's wrong, but it's hidden from their view, inside your head.

Now with your mind map in front of you, you can see what they see but in greater detail, because you know your own experiences and surroundings better than they do.

Parent Toolbox

Why not have a creative session together, to explore different ways of putting information into the various mind maps and discover which works best for each of you and why.

Also, look at the concept with them of the map – and try giving directions without knowing where you are starting and ending. Try it like a game where one of you gives directions, and the other tries to follow on the map. It can make a fun game of sorts.

I tend to list things while other people doodle them. If I asked my children to do a mind map, they were both very different in their approach.

Everyone is different and finding the right strategy for them, is more likely to create a tool that they go back to over and over of their own choice. Be creative and don't give up if the first attempts don't work. Sometimes you will need to go away and come back to exercises again at a later date.

Key Points

Starting your journey like you are starting on a map will help you in so many ways. You will see early on, how this raises your awareness, and the journey ahead may seem scary. You can ask a parent or responsible adult to help you on this journey by doing the suggestions in the parent toolboxes together. If you want company on a journey, sometimes you have to invite people along to walk beside you. Whatever happens, they cannot make the journey for you. It's YOUR journey, and if you stay behind, expecting them to go for you – then it wasn't your journey after all. They are the ones gaining the experience and growth – and that's their journey. Show up for YOU.

YOUR STARTING POINT

Now you have something to start working on; this is the START of your journey with the Mood Mentor system.

You now have a starting point. This is the map of exactly **where** you are now. This is the current moment of your journey in life. The chances are that until now, you've tootled along not really knowing how to control the steering wheel of your emotions, letting home life and school, college, or university, throw all kinds of twists and turns at you. You may have a part-time job, you may have some terrific friends, but you're still struggling for some reason.

You're probably feeling like you are following life blindly, allowing other people and circumstances to direct you. You've probably felt quite lost at times. Maybe you've completely lost your bearings altogether, and life feels like one big panic or like you're scrambling around in the dark.

Whatever you feel, don't panic! Keep reading, and you'll find your way again.

From today, you now know exactly 'where' you are. This mind map will soon help you reset your compass. The rest of this book will teach you how to identify your emotional journey and set your compass in the right direction, so you can start taking positive steps forwards.

Your first mind map will be a brilliant reference tool to use over and over. You can look back at it later and see how far you've come.

You know that feeling when you are walking and don't realise how far you've walked until you stop and look back for a second? That's the feeling you will have one day looking back at your first Mind Map.

Now put your mind map somewhere safe, and we'll move on. Next, you will start learning how to identify your current emotional territory, so you can plan those all-important first steps in taking control of your own life and your own emotions.

WARNING: Personal Understanding Ahead!

Throughout the rest of this book, I will attempt to show *how much I understand your situation*, even though we have probably never met. I have two grown children, both have suffered depression, and so have I.

Everyone is in a different situation; male, female, teen, young adult, school, work, unemployed, poor, rich, abused, loved, intelligent, learning difficulty, straight, gay - yet we all feel the same **core emotions**. The knowledge I can share with you will help a little, or a lot, regardless of your circumstances.

I need you to understand that when I'm a little off mark, it's because there are so many variants. Use your intuition, tweak the exercise a little, ask someone you trust to help, or contact me through my website or social sites. Whatever you do though – don't give up!

The challenges you face today may be different from the ancestors of the past, but how life affects your emotions and how you manage emotions are the same.

I love all these sayings, but the last one relates to the Mood Mentor Model and finding simplicity in all the chaos. The methods I developed for teaching emotional intelligence, chunk life into a handful of colours and words, so you can always find an easy starting point for overcoming any challenge.

EXERCISE 2:

DAILY REMINDER

Circle or mark the quote that you like the most from below and repeat it to yourself several times over.

Write the quote on a piece of paper and put it somewhere; you will see it every morning.

Repeat the quote every morning, to remind yourself why you are making this journey.

QUOTES FOR LIFE: "BEING ORGANISED"

"There are three things hard: Steel,
A diamond, and to know one's self."
~ Benjamin Franklin 1706 – 1790
(Founding Father of United States)

"You can't reach for anything new if your hands are still on
yesterday's junk."
~ Louise Smith 1916 – 2006
(First lady of racing – Daytona)

"Science is organised knowledge – Wisdom is organised life."
~ Immanuel Kant 1724 – 1804
(German philosopher of the mind)

"Out of clutter, find simplicity."
~ Albert Einstein 1879 – 1955
(Theoretical Physicist)

This is a simple yet powerful exercise and is used by many very successful people, to keep themselves motivated. For me, finding simplicity out of my son's cluttered mind is why I'm writing this all down for you to learn how to do the same. It really does work.

Parent Toolbox

Having a conversation that follows on from being lost is about clarifying the here and now. This helps recognise and list down – or create a new mind map – of all the good things that your teenager has, as a starting point for their journey—a bit like listing the equipment in their backpack such as water, compass, torch, map.

What do they have? Compassion? Skillsets? Favourite topic? Family or support? What every they can identify as strength, skill, or tool for their journey will empower them to see the possibilities ahead.

Key Points

Empowering is another tool that is unbelievably valuable in the parent toolbox. Imagine the difference you feel, when your partner or your manager empowers you instead of giving orders and demanding deadlines while restricting you from using strategies you think work better. Empowerment creates incredible personal growth.

RECOGNISING WHEN YOU ARE LOST

The exercise in this chapter is to read and fully understand the concept of being emotionally lost. Learn how to check in with yourself from time to time and see.

It is important to understand if you are lost now or how to recognise being emotionally lost in the future. Being able to recognise this early on in any challenge or situation gives you a head start in overcoming it. Sometimes you can even think back to times you've been lost and then found your way again. This will also help you learn to improve how you cope next time you feel lost.

My son was *very* lost. He struggled all his childhood with depression, anger and extreme mood swings. He didn't learn to manage his emotions naturally the way some people do until I created the 'emotional cycle' diagram in this book and used it to help him begin understanding emotional awareness.

My son has Asperger's Syndrome, so it took a long time for me to find a way, to teach him how to manage his emotions. I was lost. I was his mum and didn't know how to help him. I could just keep him afloat emotionally, but he kept sinking again. He needed something more, and I didn't know where to turn.

Finally, after 12 years of repeated depression, even being suicidal for many years, I finally found this way to teach him using a visual representation of his emotions. The emotional cycle diagram of the Mood Mentor Model became his map. He could finally see where he was, why he was lost, and although he didn't know the directions to where he wanted to be, it gave me a reference to work with, so I could guide him properly. Now I'm offering to guide you with the lessons in this book.

My son was in a really dark place, living in a hostel, and still feeling suicidal by the time I created the emotional cycle diagram. The changes that happened after this were incredible. This is why I want you to see incredible change too.

As I created the emotional cycle diagram and the lessons, it took about two years for my son to repeatedly implement small changes, until he finally achieved the emotional peace he was looking for. He is still learning, as learning is a lifelong habit, but he felt a sense of achievement at every step and knew when he had setbacks that it meant there were more changes to make. He was ready to face each new challenge head-on, accepting that it's a natural part of life.

You may have already learned lots about living with good and bad emotions, just being around family and friends, talking to them, mixing with strangers, watching TV, being in school or jobs, and the favourite of many young people - listening to music. Still, understanding emotions and why you have them empowers you to guide yourself more effectively.

Yes, there is loads to learn from songs and lyrics, so keep reading, and you'll even learn to appreciate your favourite artists in a whole new light.

Picking up emotional intelligence is more of a 'copying' process for most, rather than an actual understanding. It's like following someone on a journey, but you don't know the directions yourself. Therefore, when they get lost, you get lost too because you were following their guidance. You have been set examples of how to live, by the people around you. You could be following parents, teachers, managers and friends. Each of them could all be suffering depression, stress or anxiety too at times, and sometimes you can feed off their energy without realising it. Sometimes, they may be feeding off your energy.

Either way, it is time to focus on just one person right now, and that's YOU! I'll help you discover where you are, so you can see just how lost you are, or if you are

31

already ahead of the game. I'll show you how to pinpoint your location on the emotional map.

My daughter didn't have to overthink; she just learned about emotions through living her life and talking to people around her, like family, friends and teachers. She had a few stressful times being bullied because of her brother. She had teachers she didn't like and knew she had to stand up for herself and her brother and some of her friends because she had more emotional control. Later, in high school, she was bullied, and her strategies didn't work. She was lost on how to cope. Once she realised this, she could finally ask for the right help. Thankfully for her, the right teacher did help, and it stopped.

Otherwise, my daughter seemed calm, happy, and in control. Then in her late teens, when education ended, and she was job seeking, she suddenly started having panic attacks, suffering anxiety and she was facing new challenges in life and didn't know how to deal with it. She was lost again.

This is how life treats us. We just find our way; then we need to check in with the map again. We get lost again, and we find our way again. And the pattern repeats.

Although my son had the same social surroundings as my daughter, his personal needs were different. As a result, he found learning to manage his emotions as an **impossible** task. He struggled with learning anything that was a concept rather than physical reality. He found it hard to remember the days of the week. He didn't have a real sense of timing even though he could read the time on a clock. He couldn't retain numerical information such as dates, money or quantities. These are all concepts that *should* help him plan his journey in life.

Due to his Aspergers, my son had difficulty with **concepts**. He found it hard to understand the concept of his own **emotions**; therefore, having a conversation or trying to read someone else's emotions was *even more challenging.*

Lost emotionally, in the dark, scared and angry, my son refused to accept that he had Asperger's and denied being depressed. He could not see how lost he was and would not accept help for many years. He shut everyone out. Lost in his own dark place with unbearable emotions, he could not find his way out.

If you feel like this, then it is even more important that you read carefully through the rest of this book.

Only when my son finally admitted that he WAS lost and needed help, could I teach him, and he learn from me, books, life, films, music, and started seeing the lessons all around him.

Why do you need to admit when you are lost?

Sometimes you may not even realise you are lost. Imagine you are out walking and you are far from home. I want you to be in the mindset of someone downright **stubborn** for the next few minutes – DO NOT admit you are lost! YOU know where you are going, and you are certain you are going in the right direction.

Be **determined** that you are going in the right direction. Just keep walking in any direction you please. Ignore all the advice you've been given. Eventually, the road gets rough, it's dark, it's cold, you are lonely and hungry, but you're stubborn, so just keep walking even though people have stopped, called, emailed and offered to give you some different directions.

As these people pass the other way or contact you to offer help, I want you to imagine how stubborn you can really be as you tell them loudly…

- I'm a grown-up now – I can find my own way!
- I know where I'm going, I don't need your help!
- Why can't you leave me alone?

How do you feel now?

I know you need to make some journeys on your own. I know you need to learn from your own mistakes but think carefully. Do you need to make *every journey* **alone?**

I will happily let you get on with your journey but let me ask you a quick question first.

How are you going to get where you NEED to be; Not just where you think you need to be?

Stop, read each of these questions below, close your eyes, and take a minute or two to really think about the answer while you imagine being on the journey described above…

- Why do I need to know which direction I *am* walking?
- Do I have an emotional tool kit with me - in case I get *lost or hurt?*
- *Who cares* if I fall into a deep dark pit? I can climb out without help – can't I?

Do you feel different now? Are you starting to see what other people see in you? Would you begin to wonder if you really are going in the wrong direction?

OK, you can stop being stubborn now. Take a deep breath. Open your mind to your current surrounding again and take a moment to reflect on your feelings right now, today.

- Did you feel your emotions changing as you thought of being lost?
- Can you imagine how different your journey could be with proper directions?
- Can you imagine retaking the same journey with your own map, torch and compass?

That's the difference between letting life control you and learning emotional intelligence.

Emotionally, we take the same journeys and choices that we would physically. Our mind wanders just as our feet do. Our feelings stray off track just as our feet do. Our imagination leads us down the wrong path just as our feet do. You can get your life back on track, just as your feet would.

EXERCISE 3:

HOW LOST ARE YOU?

Write below, a sentence or two to describe how you feel?
Do you know exactly where you are? Are you a little off track? Or are you completely lost?

Write it in your own words:

_____

_____

_____

_____

_____

_____

_____

Parent Toolbox

If you are mentoring your teenager here rather than them reading the book, helping them reach this level of awareness is a difficult task and can initially heighten emotional states. Help them realise that they don't need to panic and that you are there to guide them.

If they don't want to read the book and you are reading it to help them, maybe just share the analogies or stories with them. Encourage them to keep talking and if it becomes too difficult in the early stages, let them cool off and try again.

Key Points

Once you can get past this point of helping them realise they are lost, you can also help them realise this isn't a bad thing. Reinforce their progress, their hopes, dreams, and talk about continuing to learn and grow. Help them realise that every step is a good step.

HITTING ROCK BOTTOM

If you've read the last chapter and feeling hopeless, and so lost that you still don't know where to turn, maybe you've got so lost, you don't know who to ask for help, or where to find help. Perhaps this is your rock bottom moment, and it's all about to get better from here.

Don't despair; this is NOT the end of your journey unless you give up. It's just time to stop, work out where you are, and figure out a plan to find your way.

Imagine you have been on that same stubborn journey, but you didn't take other people's directions and turn back. Maybe you were unlucky, and no one pointed out that you were going the wrong way.

Imagine you were so lost; you've been out there all night in the cold and dark – maybe longer.

When the sun comes up in the morning, you still feel lost and cold. You still don't know your way, and you've got no-one to ask for direction.

This is how people feel emotionally. It's just the same as in real life.

We get emotionally lost and don't know how to ask for directions.

Is it no wonder that we find it hard to talk about it, yet it doesn't have to be that hard.

- Will you let me guide you from here?
- Can I show you how to find your bearings?
- Are you ready to reset your own emotional compass?

Remember I said this book is like having a chat over a coffee table? If you're feeling low right now, why not take time to grab a drink, preferably a warm fruit or herbal tea, and let's keep chatting. Tell me anything you need by writing it down in that notebook or adding it to the Mind Map.

When you don't realise you are lost, you will keep walking further away from your emotional destination. A clue is, it's a little place called Happiness. The further you walk in the wrong direction, the further you must walk back again. If you're a long way from happiness right now, it may take longer to get back there, but... famous quote coming...

....

A journey of a thousand miles, starts with one step.
Lao Tzu

....

This is a Chinese philosopher's quote from the 6th Century B.C. and is still as relevant today, over 2,500 years later. Are you ready to take your first step with me?

I hope you now understand that it is easier to ask for help sooner than to wait until it's too late. Please don't curl up and wait for five years in this dark place the way my son did. If you already have, then I'm here now. You don't need to stay here any longer.

Once you have a map, directions, a compass, and an understanding of where you are now, you can finally plan where you are going. This will happen all in good time, but first I'm going to share a funny little story about my past.

Story

Soon after passing my driving test, I wanted to drive from Norfolk to Kent to see my grandmother. My boyfriend, at that time, came with me. I took all the directions from my father and wrote them down. My boyfriend had the map and the list of instructions. I was driving. There were no mobile phones or internet in those days, so we had a traditional paper map.

On the way there, I pretty much knew my way out of Norfolk, and I followed the road signs with my father's instructions still fresh in my head. I took a left exit at the end of the first motorway.

Once in Kent, I knew my way to my grandmother's house as it was pretty much home territory too, having lived there when I was younger.

We had a great day visiting my grandmother and one of my aunts too.

Coming back home though was a little different. That

left turn at the end of the motorway going there became an exit in the middle of another motorway coming back - and I missed the signpost. So did my boyfriend, who'd been assigned to watch for the signpost, while I was focusing on the traffic. A mini at 70mph is no match for a lorry, even when you are going the same way.

Before we knew it, instead of going through the Dartford Tunnel, we found ourselves heading towards the Blackwall Tunnel. My dad had said, if you miss one, it's not a disaster, just take the Blackwall tunnel instead. I asked my boyfriend to get the map out and re-direct us, but I didn't feel lost - yet.

This was the point where my boyfriend finally decided it was time to own up – he couldn't read a map!

He had been hoping I would just remember the way. He had no idea how to work out where we were. He couldn't find the starting point, so had no idea how to plan the journey onwards.

I was great at reading a map as I'd always read maps for my father while he was driving, but I wasn't so good at reading the signs on the route. The problem was, I was driving and couldn't pull over on the motorway, so just had to keep going.

First, it was the motorway I couldn't stop on, and then we were in Blackwall tunnel. All good so far but again I wasn't good at reading the signs. Before I knew it, we were in the wrong lane!

I couldn't change lanes as the traffic was too heavy and moving too fast, and was stuck in the left lane, the entire tunnel and out of the other end. The lane turned left, and we had to follow it. We found ourselves being forced into the middle of London City!

It all happened so quickly for me as a driver, but for him it seemed like that moment of eternity, trying to match waypoints to some random piece of paper with lines all over it, and no clue how to find the information we needed. He was giving me all the wrong directions, and I, in my panic, misread the signs.

Soon we were in one-way streets of London with traffic works and double yellow lines everywhere. I could not pull up ANYWHERE for almost an hour. We blindly drove on through the dark, and sometimes round in circles. Finally, I could stop and take the map from him to plot our way home.

I finally had the map across the steering wheel, but where was I right now? I didn't know! I was truly lost!

Let's stop to think for a minute. We'd hit **rock bottom** on our quest to find our way home! Let's look at the effects of this journey on **both our emotions.**

*It was cold, dark and getting late. Our emotions were **not happy,** and we **argued.** I was **frustrated** at what was happening and **embarrassed** at being lost. I had no one to ask directions from. He was **frustrated** at the pressure of making decisions he wasn't trained to make - and **embarrassed** at not being able to help. I was **annoyed** with myself for missing that signpost. I was **tired** as I drove home, and I felt **lost** and **drained** emotionally as well as literally.*

We had ended up much further from home than we should have. We had gone in the wrong direction. It took a while to take stock of our surroundings and locate our position on the map. Finally, we could head towards home again.

As you can imagine, our two-and-a-half-hour journey, now turned into four hours, but as Lao Tzu's wisdom says, every mile, took us one mile closer to home.

Emotional journeys are just the same as physical journeys. If you can't understand the directions your emotions are telling you, and you don't see the signs on the way, then how can you avoid getting lost, or take stock of where you are, map your emotions out, and find your way back again? This is why you are likely to hit rock bottom, and where that mind map can be a powerful tool to help you.

Can you see why hitting rock bottom is NOT the end of your journey?

Rock bottom is the moment you've realised how lost you are, and the start of your journey in the right direction.

If you're stuck in that dark place right now and can't find your way out, you may need someone to help you with this book, rather than trying to do it alone. I've been there, and my children have been there. It's much easier with a little support.

The problem is, when you call for help, parents and teachers shout down at you from their ladders of success, while friends are likely to jump in the hole with you, which is great for company, but they don't know how to rescue you, so now you're both stuck in the hole.

The few people that know how to help you out of that hole, usually have a long title and a long waiting list of about three to six months.

That's a long time to wait in the dark, and by the time you get their help, you've probably forgotten why you were sucked in that hole, and even made yourself feel at home there, or feeling you're not worth saving and no-one can help you.

Even if you are that person, start by believing there is a way out. Get that help and keep on reading.

EXERCISE 4:

DESCRIBE YOUR ROCK BOTTOM MOMENT

Maybe you're there now, been there in the past, or fear being there in the future, but write down what your rock bottom moment would be like or has been like. This helps you get it out on paper, to look back at and remember – you overcame this moment and became stronger, or can become stronger:

Write it in your own words:

_____

_____

_____

_____

_____

_____

_____

_____

_____

_____

A super important part of emotional intelligence is taking in your surroundings if you want to find your way again. Find time to sit quietly in your room, or out walking in nature, allowing our thoughts time to process peacefully. If you're always feeling sad, anxious, angry, or depressed, spending time allowing your thoughts to flow naturally in a quiet natural setting, will do your emotions a world of good. That's why children like being in the garden on a swing, or grown men like fishing by a lake, some like riding a motorbike – which my husband and I do, and it's really invigorating for the mind. Some like to do yoga or walk on the beach. Even sitting on a bench at the bottom of the garden, or by an open window with a view is better than nothing.

Pick what's available and works for you but make time to do it. As you work through this book, there will be lots of things for you to think about, and you'll need that quiet time to process your thoughts effectively.

Parent Toolbox

Helping your teenager recognise the direction they want to be heading in may be as simple as assisting them to know they are lost and letting them figure out the directions from there.

Others may need a little more support, and to work right through the book before they figure this out. Chapter two talks a lot about options, and chapter three about the keys to life. These may inspire them in ways you don't expect, so don't expect answers, just progress of any kind no matter how small is excellent.

Just getting your teenager to accept that you are proverbially holding out your hand to help, may be a massive step for some if they are frightened of what change will bring. Reward and nurture every positive moment no matter how small.

Key Points

So far, we have looked at ways of recognising your current status. Mind maps and looking lost, hitting rock bottom and becoming aware that there is an incredible journey ahead of you called life.

It's time to adventure on that journey, but first, we need to look at the signs and see what changed to bring you here. Imagine being 'there' was a place called 'Happy'. Where are you now?

Lucky for you this book breaks all these signposts down into three stages. Firstly, which emotional territory you are in terms of colour, then you will learn to read the signs of change and root causes. These are called H.E.L.P.S. and F.L.I.T.E. Let's start with the colours first.

"Sometimes, you don't know your real strengths until you come face to face with your greatest weaknesses."

Susan Gale

STEP 1: CORE EMOTIONS

This chapter is going to sound so **crazy** – it's almost unbelievable. Stick with me as I try to explain. So far, you have learned to look in some depth at your current life. Now I am going to show you how to look at your present emotions.

Even I am not an expert on anyone else's emotions, not even my son's. What I am expert at is teaching you how to understand all that noise. How to break it down and how to use it so you can take back control of your own life.

Right now, you probably don't feel much like that expert, but remember when Karate Kid was painting fences and polishing cars? It will all come together soon! If you haven't seen the film, it's one I recommend seeing.

These four emotions are each allocated a colour throughout the rest of this book. Don't worry; I'm not going to make you paint fences with them. What they do help with is seeing emotions as a colour.

From now on, you can think of them as:

Yellow	Happy
Blue	Sad
Red	Angry
Black	Depressed

Did you know, there are literally thousands of words in the English Dictionary to describe emotions?

Some sites report over three thousand emotions while I've also heard Tony Robbins mention over six thousand. That's too much to learn for most adults! Great if you going to be a therapist, author or songwriter, but why would the average teenager need to have all that knowledge? After all, you don't **choose** how you feel – or do you?

If I tell you that by using the **four** core emotions below, you could learn to *turn your life around* and manage your emotions your whole life - does that sound more interesting? The rest is simply language used to express the subtleties and dynamics of each core emotion or combinations of them.

See the diagram below, and you will see that these four core emotions are arranged in a wheel. This is the wheel that you are going to use to drive your own emotions. Learn how to steer it.

What your emotional cycle looks like.

Happy Yellow:

Why is Yellow on top? Think of those days, you say, *"I feel on top of the world."* Or, *"I'm feeling bright and sunny."* This is the place everyone wants to be, but somehow it seems out of reach to be truly happy. Some people are genuinely happy, no matter what happens. Most of us must work hard to get here. Either way, there's no reason you can't find your place here too.

Sad Blue:

Blue is to the left as in flight. You might hear someone say, *"You look a bit blue."* Blues music is about sad stories. You might describe yourself as under the weather. You may feel a little rough, like a darker blue, being all at sea. Blue also represents fear as in fear of water, flight as in a bird flapping away suddenly. These are all negative feelings usually caused something you have lost or fear losing. As you rise towards the yellow, blue becomes calm, like the surface of a still lake—a state of reflection and tranquility.

Angry Red:

Red is on the right because anger holds us back in life. Rage, hate and bitchiness are feelings that show you feel bitter towards another person or situation. These are all angry feelings. We don't have to fight to show we are angry. Even a glance at someone, showing an angry face is enough. I'm sure you've all seen that look on a teacher's face when someone is stepping out of line in class.

Depression Black:

If you feel lost in a dark place, rock bottom or stuck in a rut like your life is the pits; this is depression. It doesn't have to be clinical depression but could be long term and severe. Depression can also be temporary, such as watching something you don't like on TV – which goes away once you turn the channel over to something you like better. It could be that dreaded class that bores you to tears each week. For me, it was history.

Why Orange?

We'll get to that a bit later too. It has a significant impact on your core emotions, but we'll focus on those first.

I still believe that emotions are something we will always keep to ourselves as a very personal thing. It's impossible for someone else to fix your emotions for you. It's possible for someone else to damage your emotions even further by trying to help incorrectly. Once again, I will reiterate that you are your own expert when it comes to knowing your own emotions. That's why we are now going to work out your current emotional starting point.

Go back to you Mind Map and try to colour your words according to the cycle. If you don't know any leave them blank, as they may be to do with chapters 2 and 3.

Now count how many of each of those colours are on your map. Write your dominant colour here:

_____

Now compare your dominant colour to the core emotions.
Is there something better than expected?
Have you realised that your individual emotions are more colourful than you felt as a whole?
Why does this breakdown of colours help?

As you can see, a dominant colour on your Mind Map helps show your overall emotional starting point. It also shows you can deal with each problem as a separate journey. Remember how we talked earlier about finding where you are now? It gives you that point to set on your emotional map. It helps you see what is making you angry and sad. These are things you can begin to work on. Any areas that make you feel depressed are where you may need additional help, or you might find later in the book that you can promote these to other colours as you work out your emotions.

*We're going to check in on each of the results, then we are going to move on and start talking about changes in your life—those that **have** happened and those that **need to** happen.*

Flick between the next chapters and categories to see what information can help you understand more about your dominant emotion. Fill in that knowledge within the other chapters. I would expect you to start feeling some deeper understanding of yourself by the time you finish this exercise.

YOUR EMOTIONAL CYCLE

This chapter is just a quick introduction to the Emotional Cycle Map. The lessons are then broken down in the following chapters.

Story

*First, let's jump back to my journey through London. Imagine how different our journey would have been if my boyfriend had explained before we left, that he couldn't read a map. He didn't want the embarrassment of telling me and was hoping he wouldn't need to read the map, but I found out the hard way. Had he confided in me before the journey, I could have taught him a few ways of spotting the landmarks, showed him how to cross-reference them to the map, and given him the **power of** giving me **clear directions** to get home. Together we could have enjoyed the journey much more.*

I still struggle with reading all those signposts in time, so nowadays, my map reading skills are supported by my new driving friend, Tom-Tom.

When you feel lost it's time to stop worrying and get this book out to act as your personal, emotional Tom-Tom.

There are a couple more things I need you to understand before we start the journey about it. The emotional cycle pictured in colours is *your emotional map*. It looks like a simple diagram, but it's quite dynamic and fluid. Sometimes the colours blend a little, but first, you need to understand how to read the map in simple colours – starting with some basic lessons.

It is important to cover some subjects in more detail and take the right steps in the right order. Are you ready to get your hands on that driving wheel and start learning?

Now you understand the importance of 'learning' to read a map, let's get acquainted with YOUR emotional cycle and start thinking of this as a map too:

Are you starting to understand how you can be your own expert?

Using the emotional diagram, let's learn this concept that *you are your own expert.* I covered this in the previous chapter if you need to recap.

You will learn to pinpoint your emotions and then turn them into something positive and happier – not just because it's what is expected by your parents, teachers, friends, colleagues or managers, but because you understand *why* it's important to YOU and *how* to achieve happiness on your own terms.

According to Tony Robbins, there are over 6,000 words in the English Dictionary that describe emotions!

Is it no wonder that growing up is so difficult when there are so many feelings and emotions to try and understand? Well, don't worry, you'll only ever use a fraction of those words to describe your emotions, and I'll help you understand this using just five colours.

No matter how many words there are for emotions, they all break down into four categories. I use **yellow, red, blue and black** to map out the core emotions; then there's **orange** to represent the changes between emotions. Does that sound a little easier?

The later chapter will describe each colour as a set of emotions, but for now, I just want you to learn the simplest version possible so we can build up gradually.

Yellow is for Happy emotions.
Blue is for emotions that are thoughts, such as calmness, sadness, grief and fear.
Red is for any action-based emotions such as anger, motivation, passion and fighting thoughts.
Black is for depression, emotional overload, feeling lost, and rock bottom moments.

To keep it super simple to begin with, you can simply think of them as Happy/Sad/Angry/Depressed.

Orange is always about changes that happen between emotions. Emotions only change because *something* changed. Learning about these changes is the most important part of learning why your emotions sometimes seem out of control.

Notice the orange in the centre of the diagram? That's your inner changes. These are your thought processes, and how you can start to reprogram your thinking, for better emotional health.

The orange around the outside is outer change. This is YOUR world. These are the changes your life throws at you unexpectedly, as well as actions that you take based on those changes.

When you understand all the possible changes that can happen, and how you act or react to them, you can start to control them a little more, or at least control the way you think about them. This is why I say:

....

Mastering Life is all about Mastering Change.
Kay Reeve

....

We'll learn more about changes in the later chapters.

So that, in a nutshell, is the emotional cycle diagram, your map of life. What's so great about this diagram is, it's simple enough to remember that once you learn it, you can always carry the image in your head and work things out as you go. What it can teach you is more in-depth emotions and is truly helpful for life.

EXERCISE 5:

READING YOUR MAP

I've placed a small version of the Emotional Cycle at the beginning of every chapter for reference:

- Start by looking at the map and learning where each colour is.
- Study each colour one at a time and think about how that colour makes you feel.
- Look at the orange circles and notice that they are inside and outside the core colours.

Once you have this map in your head, we can start to learn how to read it.

If it helps, draw the map's outline a bit bigger on a piece of paper, and label or colour it, then use to make notes on as you work through the book.

What I've learnt about emotions, most therapists understand in theory, but they don't know what the emotional cycle *looks* like. They've never seen the emotional cycle as a diagram. They know how to offer therapy, help someone through specific problems, and help them learn a little about themselves, but a therapist doesn't teach you *emotional intelligence*.

At school, you are not taught emotional intelligence. Schools will say they support emotional wellbeing and that they ensure school children are 'nurtured' and provided with opportunities to grow as a person. Schools teach all the key subjects you need in life, except emotional intelligence, yet your emotions are fundamental to who you are. After all, you use them EVERYDAY. So why don't they teach this in school?

Why don't your parents teach you this? Of course… No one taught them! Some are naturally better at it than others, and a few are wiser than others, but it's not usually passed on from parents to children as a *set topic* that will help them through life.

No one is to blame for this, and it's not school's or parents fault, it's just what it is. Till now…

Imagine it like this;
Time is invisible, yet we can see it on a clock. Because a clock makes time something we can see, it can be taught to children from a young age.

Because emotions cannot be seen or drawn, they cannot be taught to children as effectively. There's no single system for teaching emotions at a young age.

Let's hope we can change that one day, but for now, you have this book in your hands, and I'm really glad.

There's nothing complicated about learning how emotions work, it will all come together soon, and it's not scientific. It just takes a little learning and a lot of practice throughout life.

YELLOW – HAPPY

What is the first thing that comes to your mind when you think of being happy?

....

Don't let the silly little things steal your happiness.
unknown

....

Sometimes you may feel like that's exactly what has happened, and that an unkind word or a bad thing has stolen your happiness. Good news is no one has stolen it, and you still have it. All of it. You are just looking at another part of the emotional cycle right now through your own mental microscope.

If you can remember anything that made you feel happy, and how excited you were or what you said, then it has not been stolen. Focus on it, and feel the changes in your emotions, even if it is temporary. Realise that you do have a choice about which emotions you focus on, but it still takes a lot of practice.

....

You can't have a rainbow without a little rain.
Dolly Parton

....

Learn to use all your emotions wisely, and you can paint any picture you want. Your life is your canvas, and you are the artist of your own emotions. Try listening to Dolly's song 'Coat of Many Colours'.

The Diagram Explained

CORE EMOTION: Happiness is a part of your emotional cycle that makes you feel light. You might refer to it as being lighthearted, on top of the world, smiling like the sun is shining, or that you are simply glowing with delight.

COLOUR: Happiness is yellow because it is a colour that is often used to describe happy words such as sunshine, flowers, fluffy ducks, golden trophies, and the warm sand beneath your feet at the beach.

PLACEMENT: Happiness is at the top of the cycle because it makes you feel light and floaty. Your moods lift, you hold your chin up, and your voice raises with excitement when you are happy. You even raise your arms as if they are tied to helium balloons when you cheer, when rushing towards a friend to greet them with a big hug, or when your football team scores the winning goal.

The Purpose Of Happiness

What happens when you stop being happy is that your emotions say *"Oh no, you're not staying there forever. Get back here! We want you to be happy."*

You say *"I'm fed up, and I just want to be happy again."*

Every person on earth is DRIVEN towards happiness, driven by that emotional cycle of four colours, and the power of change. Right now, your emotions might have changed, and you are stuck in another emotion temporarily or longer, but your happiness is still waiting for you, and it is not lost or stolen.

Also, there is a purpose for the other emotions, that call you away from happiness, and we will look at them in the other colours, but happiness is the part that tells you *"You have succeeded"* or *"You are safe"* or *"You are well fed and can stop eating."*

Meet Cave Man Dan. He has been out hunting and had to be brave. He had to be fierce. He had to be cautious, but when he caught his supper, what would happen if he was still feeling fierce and courageous? He might not feel like bringing supper home to his cave and his family.

Feeling happy was an important emotion to Cave Man Dan, to ensure that by evening, he was safe, fed, contented, and tucked up in his cave ready to sleep.

Happiness is a *sense of completion* that helps you relax and stop what you are doing so you can rest and recover to start again.

EXERCISE 6:

LIST WORDS YOU MIGHT USE TO DESCRIBE BEING HAPPY

Listing these words helps you learn to recognise your own emotions, and how you talk about them, to yourself and to other people.

_____

_____

_____

_____

_____

If Caveman Dan didn't feel happy, he probably couldn't sleep well. I bet you find it difficult to get to sleep when you're not happy too.

....

To be happy, tie it to a goal, not to people or things.
Albert Einstein

....

This is how our cavemen ancestors found happiness, by reaching goals such as finding a meal, a place to live, a mate, or lighting a fire.

Today we have those too easily, but our brain still needs goals of some kind, to use that emotional cycle correctly and find happiness each day.

EXERCISE 7:

HAPPY MIND MAP

Make a Mind Map of some of the things you *like* to do, that you can use to create happy goals in your daily life. Make them small and achievable, like listening to at least one song, or spending five minutes talking to one of your parents about something fun, running, anything that creates success in a good way.

Parent Toolbox

You may need to help your teenager recognise some of the things that make them happy, as through depression they can easily lose touch with their inner child and stop being aware of the things they do for fun.

Sometimes teenagers think something they are doing is fun, but it's not making them happy enough. They may be confusing happy with comfortable escape.

Help them explore the emotions around this, and whether they are using the activity as an escape out of habit. If they are, don't try and correct the habit at this stage, just focus on the book and ultimately finding the emotions behind it.

When we get to options in chapter two and start resolving changes behind the emotions, destructive habits should begin to resolve themselves naturally through their own choices.

SAD – BLUE

What's the first thing that comes to mind when you think of being blue?

....

You can never love someone as much as you can miss them.
John Green

....

Darkness and blue emotions are about thoughts and feeling, reflections and memories, anxiety and grief. There are no actions associated with these emotions, only alternative thinking to overcome them, transform from them, and accept them as part of your life and part of who you are. Blue emotions are the water to your flowers, but they need sunshine too to make them grow.

Like looking at your reflection in the water, or an old photograph, they are memories of the photographs of your mind and serve to help you learn from the past.

Living in the past, however, stops you living in the present. Sadness is an important part of your emotional cycle to go through, but not a place you want to stay for very long.

The Diagram Explained

CORE EMOTION: Sadness is a thought, and blue emotions are all about how *deep* you think.

COLOUR: Blue is thoughts as in air, or reflection as in water. Both sky and sea are blue and both associated with emotions and how they flow. You can fly great ideas, you can float thoughtfully on the surface, or you may put in a little extra effort to swim through a few minor difficulties. If you start to drown in your own thoughts, however, you will feel panic and anxiety. Grief or drowning in sorrow is a deep emotion where you most likely need a friend to help you out.

PLACEMENT: These thoughts, both light and dark, are one of the changes that happen between happiness and sadness. It is the key area where positive and negative thoughts lift you up or weigh you down. You are very unlikely to go directly from yellow to black and back. There is always a thought process that takes you into blue on the way up or the way down. Thoughts start high and sink deeper until grief finally drags you down into depression.

To float again lets' get that Brain Unchained!

The Purpose Of Sadness

Sadness is a horrid feeling, and yet it is really, very important. Imagine Caveman Dan went out with his family, and they saw a lion. If he didn't understand the feeling of sadness, he would not worry about their safety or his own and keep walking toward the lion.

If the lion ate one of his family, he wouldn't care because caring is a thought process. Grief is a thought process too. Without thoughts, you would not grieve or miss anyone. Neither would you feel the need to stay safe.

Blue emotions are all about staying safe. They create anxiety to keep you away from danger, but when you are feeling anxiety over something like being called names, this adds stress hormones to your body that you need to get rid of again. For Dan, this would be running away, the more afraid he was, the further and harder he would run to safety, which is why exercise is good for helping relieve stress and anxiety. Also, meditation helps your brain think you are already back at that campfire and safe again.

When you are feeling anxious or fearful, reflect why you feel this. When you know, recognise what doesn't feel safe, and talk about what you can do to feel safe again even if it is running back to your bedroom to do some more meditation.

EXERCISE 8:

LIST WORDS YOU MIGHT USE TO DESCRIBE DIFFERENT THOUGHTS AS ABOVE.

Listing these words helps you learn to recognise your own emotions, and how you talk about them, to yourself and to other people.

_____

_____

_____

_____

_____

_____

_____

_____

_____

_____

_____

_____

_____

_____

_____

_____

Any fool can be happy. It takes a real man to make beauty out of the stuff that makes us weep.
Clive Barker

Example

This is how people take the rainy days and make the flowers grow, by thinking positive and acknowledging that even the most beautiful flowers need a little rain sometimes.

EXERCISE 9:

SAD MIND MAP

Make a Mind Map of some of the things that make you sad, anxious, or that you find yourself reflecting on most often. Think about how these thoughts keep you safe and have a purpose, or how you may need strategies to reduce the thoughts that are less helpful.

Parent Toolbox

Helping a teenager acknowledge what thought processes they may be going through could be challenging for them to begin with, in opening-up. Be there to listen to whatever they say and hold all judgement and solutions at this point.

It's purely about getting the conversations going as you work through the book that will ensure greater success moving forward. It may also be helpful through all these exercises to make your own notes about how your teenager uses these emotions, words and patterns, to see if you can spot something that may help them raise emotional awareness in themselves.

ANGRY – RED

What is the first emotion that comes to mind when you think of the colour Red?

....

Fight for what you love and do whatever it takes to be happy.
Unknown

....

Yes, you might think love, passion or motivation, while I've said that red is about anger, but they are all on the same wavelength except love is the positive version of hate. Passion is the positive version of aggression. Anger is about fighting, even if you only think it in your mind, but loving someone or loving what you do, will make you fight for it, even in words, looks or actions.

Red is about action – words and thoughts that are associated with doing.

The Diagram Explained

CORE EMOTION: Red emotions are anger and hitting out physically or lashing out verbally. Red is about doing, or saying, as speaking is an action. This can be through bitchy comments, words of hatred, fighting, being pushy, or even aggressive. More positive varieties of doing or saying, are passion and motivation through speaking compliments. Even if you only think hatred, it is still aimed 'at' something or someone.

COLOUR: Red is used to describe red-mist when someone reaches pure anger and loses sight of all other emotions in the moment. Red rag to a bull describes antagonising someone else to make them angry. Boxing gloves are mostly red, symbolising fight and power. Hearts are not just about love but can be broken too, and either way symbolises external connections with another person, you are willing to fight for, or the anger of a broken relationship.

PLACEMENT: Red is the other route between happy and depressed. When something makes you angry, and you cannot resolve it, you get more and more angry until you sink to aggression and possible crime, or you cross over to grief at losing the fight and try to think your way out. If you still don't resolve it, you get stuck between the two in fight or flight mode, and eventually, depression takes over.

More positively, motivation leads to happiness, especially when there is a goal to work towards and a reward that brings more joy to success. This is why sports are so popular because it drives motivation towards winning the trophy and success equals happiness.

Key Points

You will find emotions switching a great deal between red and blue, but the aspect of keeping everything positive means that when switching between the higher emotions, you go through happiness. In comparison, the lower emotions cross through depression. Look at the chart and try to trace the emotional switches from side to side, and see what I mean.

The Purpose Of Anger

Would you believe it that anger also helped Cave Man Dan every day?

Imagine this time he has speared a deer for supper. That pesky lion is back but is about to steal the deer. Dan will probably think fear and stay safe because he has to weigh up his options of going hungry or being eaten alive.

But what if it was a basket of berries instead, and a cheeky chimpanzee was trying to steal his fruit? Now he has a chance of not going hungry, so he will get angry at the chimpanzee and chase it away to claim his rewards.

Whether Dan gets angry or not, depends on his inner thoughts about his own abilities to fight. If he thinks he can't fight, it will be because of fear, and he will stay safe – but hungry. He will just have to hunt again. If he thinks fighting is safe – he won't go hungry.

Using this thought process will help you work out what you can do to take actions from chapter two, about finding your hunger for life again.

EXERCISE 10:

LIST WORDS YOU MIGHT USE TO DESCRIBE FEELING ANGRY

Listing these words helps you learn to recognise your own emotions, and how you talk about them, to yourself and to other people.

_____

_____

_____

_____

_____

The pessimist sees difficulty in every opportunity.
The optimist sees opportunity in every difficulty.
Winston Churchill

Example

Whatever you are fighting for, working towards, passionate about, or have hatred for, you will find what you are looking for. When you train your mind to be looking for positivity and opportunities instead of difficulties, you will naturally find your way to a happier life.

EXERCISE 11:

ANGRY MIND MAP

Make a Mind Map of some of the things that make you angry or frustrated, or that you find yourself thinking of saying to others. Think about how these thoughts have a positive purpose, or how you may need strategies to reduce the thoughts that are less helpful to you and others.

Parent Toolbox

Dealing with anger can be one of the most difficult emotions when a teenager is prone to tantrums, but many have inner anger that they bottle up. Dealing with this anger is necessary to move upwards through the emotional cycle; otherwise, it persistently holds them down. Help them realise the power of other ways of thinking as options.

You may need to come back to this section repeatedly for an angry teenager to work through all their triggers one at a time. Repeatedly doing this will build better habits as they are unlikely to shift all thinking overnight.

BLACK – DEPRESSED

What does the colour black mean to you emotionally?

....

***Depression is in part, grief for your own life not turning out
how it should, grief for your own needs not being met.***
Johann Hari

....

Depression is a dark place to be. It feels cold and lonely, hard to see a way forward, and is often referred to as 'stuck in a rut' or 'at rock bottom' or you might say 'I feel like I'm in the pits' or even 'there's no light'.

There are other ways people talk about depression too, but they are always linked to the colour black or being in darkness. It feels heavy and even though people say 'we're here for you', you can't see it. Your head just wants to shut down, you want to close the door, and you feel like hibernating away from everyone and everything.

The Diagram Explained

CORE EMOTION: Depression is harder to fight and feels like being chained down. Teenagers in depression are afraid to face up to their emotions because trying to do so makes them sad or angry. Having read about red and blue emotions, you can now understand why it's easier to sit and hide in the dark than to face up to your emotions, but now you know, to make those choices and ask for help to find your way back to the light.

COLOUR: Black is associated with loss, hopelessness, lack of light, and the darkness of being in the pits, or stuck at rock bottom. It is the colour of death, and often the colour depressed teenagers revert to wearing to reflect their emotions.

PLACEMENT: Depression is like the gravity end of the emotional cycle. Gravity is heavy compared to that happy helium balloon that floats on its own. Just as happy is positive, black is the negative end of the emotional cycle and can leave you feeling like that battery drained of all energy, yet depression still has a positive purpose in a small way.

The Purpose Of Depression

We're going to revisit Caveman Dan as he's in need of help.

Imagine he woke up this morning and it's snowing a blizzard. Mammoths are stampeding around the valley outside. He's got some food leftover from yesterday, a bit of a fire, and enough water for a few hours.

Dan knows that to go outside today will leave him feeling really cold, and dangerous trying to cross through the stampede to get some wood. He's also got a headache, and his feet still hurt from yesterday's hunt.

Dan's emotional cycle has moved into self-protection mode today, and he feels depressed. His emotions are telling him that the best thing to do today is to stay put. The depression makes it easier for him to preserve energy and remain in the cave.

Imagine if Dan tried to stay in and was feeling angry like hunt mode. What if he felt fear? That wouldn't serve him any purpose beyond recognising the mammoths are well… mammoth. He knows it, so he doesn't need to feel that fear all day as he is safe in his little cave.

Being happy would encourage Dan to want to do something fun, but he can't go out, and there's not much in the cave. Instead, he sets back into a mini depression to save energy and sit the storm out by his little fire, and probably sleep more to let his achy body heal.

When your brain gets overloaded with problems, like Dan's winter day, your brain takes you back to your cave, and you curl up in bed to sleep. Some days this is great as your body and brain need a rest. The only problem is, if you're stuck here you haven't learned how to get back out of that mode, and back to setting new goals for a new day.

LIST WORDS YOU MIGHT USE TO DESCRIBE FEELING DEPRESSED.

Listing these words helps you learn to recognise your own emotions, and how you talk about them, to yourself and to other people.

_____

_____

_____

_____

You only live once but if you do it right, once is enough.
Mae West

Example

This book should help you start living your life right. It may sound crazy talking about your emotions compared to a caveman, but the emotional cycle, in a world filled with change, is the one thing that hasn't changed since the days of Caveman Dan.

Every human today tries to adapt their emotions to our new world filled with complex societies, sciences, politics, war, religion, culture, technology and more, without giving it a thought as to what their caveman brain still wants – to make them happy. This is why the great outdoors is so powerful.

Embrace your inner caveman to help you become a better human being today.

EXERCISE 13:

DEPRESSED MIND MAP

Make a Mind Map of some of the things that make you feel down, depressed, or simply needing a day to recoup. Think about how you embrace these days as positive recovery days, or whether you are stuck in your cave and need new emotional strategies for breaking free again.

Parent Toolbox

Teenagers in depression are afraid to face up to their emotions because trying to do so makes them sad or angry. Having read about red and blue emotions, you can now talk to them about the importance or the helpfulness of doing this, plus you are now equipped with the knowledge to hold their hand through this journey rather than let them face the fear and the anger alone.

This is where you shine that torch for them every single day, till they can find their own way at last.

CHANGE - Orange: Orange is about inner and outer changes and why you change between emotions. It helps you discover what already changed and what your options are for positive change.

The inner and outer orange circles create the second part of the emotional awareness system and the whole of Chapter Two H.E.L.P.S. you understand these changes, but first, let's look at positive and negative emotional awareness.

POSITIVES VS NEGATIVES

$\mathbf{A}$s I talked through the colours of the positive and negative effects of emotions, I hope you started to realise there are three options at any point on the map. You can move up the diagram towards more positive emotions, down the diagram towards negative emotions, or stay where you are stuck.

The Diagram Explained

Positive is at the top of the emotional cycle, and negative is at the bottom. Like positive and negative, your emotions are FULL of happiness or DEVOID of emotion at the very top and bottom of this cycle. Everything in between is like the map of your emotions.

If you choose not to think positively or say 'that doesn't work' then you are by default choosing to think negatively or to stay where you are. Now that you realise that, why would you choose negative?

We talked about blue emotions like sadness and anxiety, and there are times where thinking these are important to staying safe or avoiding loss but be careful not make this a bad habit, for not trying to be positive.

Think of being happy like being a bird. When you are positive and happy, you feel like you can fly, but that also means you constantly have to flap your wings or you fall from the sky again.

That's why staying happy requires effort. No one can party forever. You burn out, feel worn out and still have to go through the other emotions to recover.

You need to use all the emotions properly, just as Caveman Dan, to really live a full and happy life. This means life takes turns left and right into the red or blue emotions but depending on how far up the diagram you are, this will change the outlook and the actions you take.

EXERCISE 14:

LIST WORDS YOU MIGHT USE

Listing these words helps you learn to recognise your own emotions, and how you talk about them, to yourself and to other people.

Analogy

Your brain, however, works more like a cycle – an emotional cycle to be truthful, and like a cog in a clock, your brain needs to keep turning to keep ticking. Your current emotional state is like the hand that keeps coming back round to 12 o'clock so it can chime again. For some people, having routines is important to achieving this, or they feel they just cannot function.

Explanation

By knowing about the cycle and then treating the emotional diagram like a map for your emotional journey, you can follow your journey to learn your patterns, and then learn to guide your journey that way you want to go.

You can laugh and play, then reflect happy thoughts about the day you had, then rest a bit or meditate to allow your inner thoughts to take over while you sleep.

You can then set new positive actions for the next day, and keep this happy cycle going as long as possible. You don't have to go all the way to the bottom of the map to go through yellow, blue and red.

Try drawing the map out roughly, then draw the smallest path that encompasses yellow, some of the red and blue, some outer change and some inner change for each colour, but avoid the line going into or around the black. This is a healthy emotional cycle. Your path will look like this...

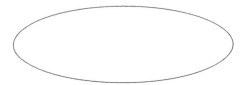

Many teenagers have got lost and are doing the same oval route, like walking round and round the sports track, but their oval route is drawn across the bottom of the emotional cycle, in difficult terrain. They feel sad, angry and depressed - and no matter how much they try, there just seems no way out.

There seem to be no doors opening. No light at the end of the tunnel. If this is you, be grateful right now, that you have a book in your hands that will show you the way out, and how to re-draw that map at the positive end of the emotional cycle again.

If you are in depression at the bottom of that route and follow it sideways towards red, you are likely to feel angry. If you move towards blue, you feel completely overwhelmed and find yourself crying without knowing why you're sad. Being at the bottom of the cycle in depression is no longer about resting; it is about feeling unsafe.

If you are feeling unsafe, get help and don't walk this part alone but don't give up either. You now have the knowledge to work through this.

Keep reading but share the reading with someone if it helps you.

Taking steps from here is *still thinking positive* because the only way is up, literally. It's facing up to your emotions, but you have to work through them first. It will take a little while to redraw your map because you need to make changes, which you will learn about in chapter two.

When these kinds of feelings set in, this is like Caveman Dan going through those winter feelings and retreating to his cave to sit out the storm. You're just going through an emotional storm. Use this time-out in your mind to do some sit-ups or doodle pictures, play music, or something else that helps your mind relax before you start setting small goals again but remember to make it a positive thought to do those things 'for you'.

How you think, feel and believe, will make the choice for you between red and blue emotions as you work through your emotional map. This is the reason it is important to use those emotions carefully and express them safely when you are feeling depressed, one step at a time.

If you are naturally drawn towards anger the way my son was because he wanted to 'do something' to put his world to rights, you will need to do it by running, or boxing, martial arts, or anything that gives you a positive physical outlet.

If however your mind is drawn to sad thoughts and you find yourself crying, this is good, let it out and work through it. If you keep crying over and over, but not coming through the sadness, you may need a counsellor to help you work out why you feel that way, to begin with.

If you are still struggling to work through the anger or sadness, there may be a cog stuck in your thoughts and beliefs – called cognitive thinking - which a friend, therapist, teacher, or counsellor can help you mend and heal so you can start ticking over on your own again. Don't feel you have to work it out alone.

Therapy is not a stigma; it's a conversation with someone more experienced and knowledgeable about emotions, who can help. You can get some help by asking your doctor, or by contacting a local charity.

Many other days, you will know that this feeling of depression is only temporary because you are your own expert. You will know what happened, such as a friend being mean, your parents saying you can't have new trainers yet, your homework being marked lower than you hoped, or not feeling well in winter. Maybe it's the third time your sports team has lost a game. Be grateful for somewhere safe to go and enjoy the storm quietly, whether it's your bedroom or the local library.

Find your safe place to watch the storms pass.

....

And once the storm is over, you won't remember how you made it through, how you managed to survive. You won't even be sure whether the storm is really over. But one thing is certain. When you come out of the storm, you won't be the same person who walked in. That's what the storm is all about.

Haruki Murakami

....

Example

When you learn to embrace positive and negative thinking for the right purpose at the right time, this is called resilience, and building strengths. What you go through, you grow through. You learn, and you become stronger.

EXERCISE 15:

STRENGTHS MIND MAP

Make a Mind Map of all the things in your life that are your personal strengths. Physical strengths, even if it's the ability to walk. Emotional strengths like listening to a little sister when she's sad too, or skills such as playing the guitar, or your best topics from school. Your dreams are also strengths because you have goals to focus on. Write it all down and list all the things that are waiting at that positive end of your emotional cycle.

Parent Toolbox

Sometimes you may be saying and doing all the right things, and your teenager is just struggling to connect with you or understand what you are trying to help them with. This book should help overcome that barrier.

Helping any teenager think positively and recognising negative habits can take lots of practice and positive reinforcement because often their habits have been the result of inheriting thoughts and beliefs from the people around them. It may also need you to look at how other siblings in the family think, and how you hold conversations between all of you as a family.

It is not intended for you to reflect badly on the past - as shame or guilt hold no purpose - but learning and growing as a family holds boundless possibilities for you all. As an author, I must acknowledge that for some teenagers, their depression is because of the family setting. A parent may also be in depression and unable to assist their child until they help themselves first, or abuse may be taking place.

Also check with your child discretely in conversation *alone*, if another person is abusing them in any way.

Key Points

Sometimes teenagers are too scared to say they are being abused because of the consequences of threats an abuser can make against a parent. An abusive father, for example, might say, *"If you tell your mum, I'll kill her and you."*

An abuser will use negativity and fear against their victim to keep their own manipulated world positive and in their control. They know the teenager might be suicidal as a result of the abuse, but will use their compassion for a parent to instil fear.

If you are that teenager reading this, and in that situation, then you must speak to a teacher, manager, doctor, or police, to get help. You can also call the Samaritans or Childline. There are some phone numbers at the end of the book.

You must ask them to take you somewhere safe. Don't let this abusive person keep destroying your life - because they are emotionally sick and twisted. If they do this to you, they have the mental health problem, not you.

....

Love yourself enough to get help – now.

....

If and when your life is safe, and you recognise that your emotions are your emotions only, then it's time to look forward and start learning about how emotions change and what you can do to start taking control of your own life.

"Sometimes we don't know our strengths until we come face to face with our greatest weaknesses."

Susan Gale - Author

STEP 2: CHANGE

Options are having a choice when something changes. Do you feel like your parents are constantly telling you how to live your life? Are you faced with so many options you feel lost?

If so, this may be their way of trying to help you cope with the changes of moving into adult life. They merely want to share their experience, but you know that life had also changed since they were teenagers. As a result, you become at loggerheads with each other but trust me, don't write them off yet.

Have you considered that your parents are trying to help you learn about change but do not know how else to explain it?

Instead, they say things like;

> "There's light at the end of the tunnel."
> "It's just a stepping stone."
> "You can get yourself through this."
> "Grow up and act your age."

It can feel overwhelming, but parents do not know how else to help you, so cut them a little slack, try and connect with them about the book if you can.

The one thing your parents do understand is that the light does exist at the end of the tunnel when you come out of depression and reconnect with life. What they don't know is what the map of 'your' tunnel looks like. They don't know how to shine the torch for you to find the way. But I do, and I did it for my son.

Matthew found his way to the lighter side of life and said it felt like his brain had become unchained. Hence the title of the book.

This book can help bring you and your parents back in line with each other by understanding *your* options through the following part of the Mood Mentor Model and why they were trying to share what *they* see as your options, to help you.

Your Options

Everything that happens in life is some form of change. Understanding the sheer number of changes that occur all the time, and how they impact our emotions, can also help you turn those changes around once you know your options. I will cover this more in chapter two, but for now, I just want you to think about the fact that you have more choices than you may think.

Just let your awareness begin here.

Change

Getting up is a change from being in bed. Getting dressed is a change of clothes. Eating is the change from being hungry to being satisfied. Each of these are options as well.

On a Saturday, you may have the option to stay in bed longer, lounge in pj's and eat something other than a quick bowl of cereals, or avoid that comfort eating a little longer. These are all options that most people take for granted.

When you face more significant life changes, it often helps to look at the change in the same way. You have exam subject options at school. You have the option to learn to drive. You have the option of who you hang around with and keep in your social circle.

You can also make changes to each of these at any time too.

You can change the subject, or you can change your career at any time of life. Knowing this makes choosing a career less daunting. Now you can focus on the career you want to *begin* adult life with, and worry about the rest later. You can change your driving license and take an advanced test, or even learn to drive a lorry. Changes are always available. You can also lose your license if you don't drive safely.

You can change who you have as friends and let toxic people step away while surrounding yourself with more positive people who make you feel good.

Change is constant in this world, and you can use the energy of change to your benefit once you understand that changes are not as complicated as you think.

This chapter will help you understand the only five changes in the whole world, that you can face.

Challenge

Taking changes in life and turning them into a challenge is considered more of an art form, but it doesn't have to be. Everyone can turn life's changes into challenges with a bit of effort and practice.

What if you've put on a bit of weight and your wardrobe needs changing? You can upgrade your wardrobe, or you can challenge yourself to lose weight.

Many people have made big challenges out of trauma too. People who have lost limbs, have challenged themselves to walk again, play sports, and even run marathons. What happened to them was a massive change and one they couldn't change back by growing new limbs, but what was more important to them was knowing and understanding their options to turn it into a challenge.

Challenge = Success = Happy!

This is the difference between a negative and a positive mindset. By challenging themselves in sports, they really challenged themselves to be happy again.

What's most important is that you don't challenge the changes in your life by fighting them. Challenging them is much more rewarding when done correctly.

Choice

Every change that happens to you may be a setback that you don't know how to overcome or a good change that you are happy about and accept, but whatever changes you face, you still have a choice.

You can choose whether you challenge or accept change. You can choose to give up. You can choose to be better, not bitter. You can choose to overcome grief, change career, go back to school, drop out of college (only if it's the right choice though) or you can choose to be at peace with yourself.

When my daughter was about six, we had a conversation about behaviour and talked about the film "The Little Mermaid". When I spoke of Ariel being good, my daughter exclaimed that Ariel was the bad person and the witch was the kind lady who tried to give her the legs she wanted.

I explained that the witch forced Ariel to sign the contract. My daughter said she still had the choice not to sign it and stay in the sea. Instead, she chose to sign it, get her legs and when she didn't like the deal, she killed the witch!

To this day, I cannot argue that my daughter has a strong sense of choice and that Ariel made some terrible choices, indeed.

Accept

Sometimes life makes changes we can't undo, and we can't challenge, such as losing someone you love, like a parent or grandparent, or your parents divorcing. These are changes that are super emotional but can't undo them. There's nothing you can do to challenge them either.

At times like this, you may feel out of options, and as a result, grief and anger can easily set in. This is ok to some degree, as you wouldn't feel human if you didn't cry over losing someone, or angry at your parents arguing and one of them leaving, but it is still important to talk about these changes and what you can do to feel better in time.

Acceptance is not always the quickest way to deal with negative emotions, but it is the strongest way to deal with them if you genuinely want to heal emotionally. These are times when it is beneficial to talk to someone outside the family, who is experienced in helping you through difficult emotions so you can accept the changes and transform your life to accept the good things and memories you had while they lasted.

There are also many changes that happen where acceptance is easier, such as being told you are going on holiday to Spain instead of France, or that you have a new manager at work. You may like your friend's new hairstyle, or the new brand of hot chocolate your mum started buying. Some things are easier to accept, but practising the concept of acceptance also helps you accept and process more difficult changes when needed.

Why Change Is Important

Think back to the four colours of emotions, happy, sad, angry and depressed. Each is important, and each has a purpose. You also know that you change between emotions, but do you know why?

The answer is shorter than you may think.

The only reason you change between emotions is because something changed.

Take a few minutes to reflect on that statement. What changes have you faced that changed your emotions?

Let's look back again when your parents did everything for you. As a baby, they made all the changes for you. This might be step-parents, carers or other family, but the principle is always the same.

You started life by crying when things changed. You cried when you became hungry, or your nappy became wet or dirty. Your parents made the necessary changes to make you feel better again by feeding you when you were hungry or changing your nappy when you pooped.

Imagine if your parents had made the wrong changes and hung toys on your pram to stop you crying when you were really hungry or wrapped you in a blanket to keep you warm when you were already too hot. This would not be helpful at all.

You change every day, and parents have to change with you from baby to adult - but sometimes you both become lost in those changes. Remember that chapter on getting lost?

Growing up doesn't just happen. Change happens your whole life. You gradually learn to do different things for yourself while your parents or family make changes to stop doing them for you, like getting dressed, reading your own bedtime stories, through to getting your own mobile phone, learning to drive.

This could also be doing your own homework or getting a job and earning your own money. Have a thoughtful moment here, that with every change in *your* life, your parents had to make changes too. It's not just you that feels that change and the pressure. It's not only you that doesn't always know how to communicate what changes you need.

Just as your life gets more complex; your parents also find helping you more complex. This is why many teenagers and parents fall out and argue, but with the knowledge in this chapter, you can make that connection another change for the better.

- What if you have been unfortunate and don't have that parental support?
- What if you don't have someone to teach you how to progress into adult life?
- How to cope with hormonal changes, leaving school, working, learning to love?

How do you learn to manage your emotions when living in a house of emotional turmoil, neglect or even abuse?

The answer is the same. Read and learn about change, then adapt it to your situation so you can get the help you need.

You cannot change the past, but we can learn from it – good or bad, and you can choose which lessons – good or bad, create positive changes for the future. I will talk more about when help is needed, a bit later.

....

Mastering Life is all about Mastering Change
Kay Reeve

....

The Diagram Explained

On the Emotional Awareness diagram, you can see two sections that are orange. Inside and outside. These represent the changes that happen in you and the changes that occur around you. They can help you move between emotions positively or negatively. These changes also connect your thoughts, feelings and beliefs, with the actions you take when change happens around you.

Right now, take a few moments to think... can you imagine your life, if nothing ever changed? NOTHING. Not good or bad. Just nothing. Which emotion would you like to be stuck in if nothing ever changed?

You will learn in this chapter, why *CHANGE* is the most important word you will learn in your whole life, why you need change as much as you need air and water. It is time to start discovering that chain that wraps around your brain and prevents emotional freedom. It is also time to learn how to begin unlocking it and feel the freedom of **Brain Unchained**.

Remember, we talked in Chapter one about Positive and Negative? Changes are the force behind both positive and negative moments in yourself and in the way you think. These changes can create fear and anxiety, stress, anger and frustration. Changes can also make you happy, thoughtful, and enlightened, to name just a few of the feelings that happen with change.

Once you get the word 'Change' embedded in your mind as the choices that you have over *your* life, you will start to hear it as a daily power word. You will hear it in conversation, on the news, in films, in songs, and in every motivational video you can find.

Change will jump out at you. It meets you at every turn in life, becoming your best friend and worst enemy in one. Knowing which one is which, will help you make the right choice as many times as possible.

The Purpose Why Emotions Change

It is the change in your friendships that make you happy or sad. Your exam results change your opportunities while your diet and exercise levels change your physical body. Change is the driver of everything you will ever do or have happen to you.

EXERCISE 16:

LIST YOUR CURRENT CHANGES

Well done, that's a lot of reading about change so far. Let's stop a minute so you can start listing some words you might use to describe changes in your life.

_____   _____

_____   _____

_____   _____

_____   _____

Analogy

> Time to check in on Cave Man Dan and see how his hunting went today. We spoke earlier about how he woke up, picked berries, then later went hunting to gather food for his family.

Can you imagine if Dan didn't feel the changes in his body as he became hungry?

> Imagine what would happen if he just sat by the fire, if he was smart enough to light one, and his emotions didn't change from that yellow happy place at the top of the diagram.

> Instead, Dan's story is about his awareness and recognising why his emotions change from peaceful and happy, to being alert and focused so that he leaves the comfort of his fire to go out hunting.

> As Caveman Dan gets hungrier, he gets angrier – or

Hangry as we call it today. A change in blood-sugar-levels causes this, but Dan doesn't know that.

Remember the story about why anger was important in hunting? He changes between emotions because something changed. Dan became hungry, and his emotions changed to hangry to help him find food and hunt it down.

Just as Dan's emotions change with hunger, so do many other emotions change because of things that change in your life. Things a home, at school, at work if you already have a job. We will cover more about the many types of change in Chapter two, so you can discover when change H.E.L.P.S. you and when it becomes a barrier.

Explanation

Imagine those times when you start to feel hungry, but you are so happy what you are doing, or so focused on it, that the hunger gets ignored. You keep doing what you enjoy, but your body gets more and more hungry because your emotions didn't change.

Then when you finally get so hungry that you have to stop, you feel angry, but it's really the hunger making you angry, not that you have to stop doing what was fun. If you stayed happy, and you just kept ignoring that hunger forever, you would starve. So your hunger has to change too. It has to YELL at you to EAT!

Dan would have felt that experience around the campfire, but for you, it might be having to get off the games console because Mum called that dinner is ready. You may have been focused on your homework or chatting online to a friend.

Next time you feel like shouting at your Mum, or your girlfriend because you have to stop doing something – STOP and THINK instead… Are you shouting because your body is hungry and you are trying to ignore it?

There are many reasons we go through emotional changes, but just having this awareness will help you to start thinking more about changes in emotions and what causes them.

Keep reading, there is so much to learn, and you are doing an amazing job so far!

....

The greatest discovery of all time is that a person can change his future by merely changing his attitude.
Oprah Winfrey.

....

Analogy

When my son became aware of this concept, that life is full of change, but the power of change was his choices in response. His attitude towards making choices and taking control over his options changed enormously too.

He started backing away from toxic friends, reading more self-help books, dressing more confidently, taking care of his hygiene, and most importantly of all, connecting with people around him that could help him move forward and embrace life, instead of hanging around with people who held him back.

Within one year, he transformed from being completely depressed and suicidal, living on £25 a week, to having his own flat, a full-time job and being engaged.

EXERCISE 17:

LIST SOME OF YOUR BARRIERS

Write down some things in your life that you would like to change, but don't think you can.

_____

_____

_____

_____

Parent Toolbox

As Matthew's mum, it took me a long time to find a way to help Matthew understand all these concepts of change, but you now have the power in your hands to learn this firstly for you, and to pay it forward piece by piece, working with your son or daughter to work through one change at a time.

I wouldn't recommend trying to teach all this in one hit if your teenager is struggling with stress, anxiety or depression, but start by working on one or two small issues or challenges, and pick sections of the book to work with as needed.

Begin by helping them explore the areas of life where they already have the power to make their own changes, and become aware of the chains that hold them in.

Over time, your teen will start to find their flow and can continue to come back to these lessons at any time in life. It doesn't explain the universe, but it explains the pattern they can begin to apply. Like a telescope to the universe, just look through it and focus on one small area at a time. How can they change that focus by recognising the power of change, and the options that are theirs to decide?

INNER CHANGE

This is when something changes directly within you. It could be you have a headache, feeling bored, put on weight or learned something new. Whatever it is that changed, it affects you because of your own changes. It could also be changes that happen to you because of external causes. Maybe you had an accident with a car and broke your leg. The car is an external change that happened to you, while the injury to your leg is also external to your health. How you feel emotionally about your leg is an internal change. This will make more sense as you move on.

Remember when you were little, and couldn't wait for the postman on your birthday? Now, look at how your parents have changed and how the postman has them saying *"Ugh! More bills to pay."* or *"Ugh! More junk mail!"*

Inner change is the next step of awareness, in separating all the changes we've talked about so far, into two parts. It's looking at what's happened in the world around you but exploring how you feel about it inside.

The postman still delivers letters, but your parent's or maybe even your feelings have changed. Feelings have changed towards the postman, not because he has changed, but because the type of letters he delivers has changed. It's recognising these inner feelings that help you recognise where you begin to feel unneeded stress and are aiming at the wrong person or situation.

....

Everyone thinks of changing the world, but no one thinks of changing himself.
Leo Tolstoy

....

The Diagram Explained

When you look at the internal change on the Emotional Awareness diagram, you see that the orange centre links to all four emotions. You have the power at any time, to *'change'* how you think about things by being more positive.

If you are already paying your own bills, you can practice this positive thinking now, or prepare for when you will have to do this yourself. Maybe even help your parents to feel better about it too.

You can choose to be more positive about those bills landing on the doormat and making sure you pay them on time. You can choose to become angry and frustrated at them and phone up the companies to complain about what they are charging you. You can choose to feel sad and say you don't have enough money to pay for them.

You can also choose to be happy and grateful that you have a home where the letters can be delivered, and the money to pay the bills. If this isn't the case, you can choose to set this as a goal – to become financially independent enough to achieve this, just as we talked about in turning life into challenges.

When you choose to use the core emotions in your brain to recognise how these things make you feel, and then look at the inner change, you can choose to make those changes in the way you think, before making changes to the outside world.

The Purpose Of Inner Changes

So many people blunder and plough their way through life, focusing on the outside world, angry at everything, blaming everyone, living life stressed to the max and ultimately becoming toxic to the people around them. These are people who do not understand the power of their inner changes.

The person who looks at the outside world and decides to be better, act appropriately, be grateful, helpful, thoughtful, maintain their integrity, and surround themselves with likeminded people, build strong, lasting friendships and enjoy life more, even though they could be going through the same problems as the first person. This is especially relevant when starting a job.

Two people could be working side by side, but one hates the job and the wages, complains about the government and the management. In contrast, the other person is grateful to have the job, the income, and a purpose, as well as feeling like a valued part of the company. The difference is an inner change.

EXERCISE 18:

LIST WORDS YOU MIGHT USE

What words do you use, that reflect your inner thoughts? Do you use words like can't, won't, hate, useless? Or do you use words like thoughtful, grateful, happy, purpose, or something else? Just think about now and look back at these later when you've made some changes to your personal development. It will help you look back at your progress.

_____

_____

_____

_____

_____

I'll tell you something a little different this time. An actual story of me trying to write this chapter...

I really challenged myself on this concept of change when I realised this...

It seems like we change from being perfectly happy to being bored senseless, frustrated and even angry at times because *nothing* changed. But I said earlier that we change between emotions *because* something changed. So what am I missing?

You might hear me say *"I have been doing the same job so long, it has become boring."* But how can my inner emotions change when nothing else changed?

I was about to give up on my theory of inner change when I realised this:

When I am bored, something *did* change – *I had changed*. It was my way of thinking, my expectations, my knowledge or my experiences that had changed *internally*.

When I become bored because nothing seems to have changed - what really changes is;

- My initial excitement became routine – that's change.
- My expectations became disappointment – that's change.

It's the *changes* in the way I **think** or **feel** that became the problem when nothing else changed.

On realising this, I stuck with the colour orange and the theory of change, knowing it works perfectly, without having to change my system; pardon the pun.

Explanation

Last night I was doing a live discussion on Facebook with a friend who has sight loss. His vision means that even during lockdown, he was not only stuck at home alone but couldn't even look out of the windows.

His sight had changed when he was eight years old, but as a grown man, he had chosen to be positive inside and make life fun regardless. He travels the country with his guide dog, and talks to groups of people who have the same condition of Macular Degeneration, to inspire them to be more positive too.

He obviously struggles with the loss of sight and life is different, but to him, it is still a life worth living.

....

If you have good thoughts, they will shine out of your face like sunbeams, and you will always look lovely.
Roald Dahl

....

Example

Having positive thoughts helps you feel amazing on the inside. It takes practise, but it won't happen if you don't try. When you truly find your inner positivity, it really does show from the outside. People will recognise this in you and will say things like *"You look like you're glowing."* Or *"You look like you've just won the lottery."*

When people say positive things back to you this way, it raises your self-esteem and confidence even further. The more confidence you have, the more positive you will feel and the more you will glow with happiness. Instead of a vicious cycle, you will now feel the benefits of expanding your personality and shining a light on the world.

When you shine a light on the world this way, the world and all the people around you will want to be around you and will enjoy being in your company. They will also be there for you more in times of need because they have believed in you and your powers to grow.

This is the power that you hold in you when you choose to make positive inner changes and grow from all of your experiences, good and bad.

EXERCISE 19:

YOUR INNER CHANGES

Try taking some time to write down some of the positive things that you already said. What challenges do you like to face head-on and enjoy the process involved as if it was a passion?

_____

_____

_____

_____

_____

_____

Also, write down some challenges that you find difficult and would like to improve on by becoming more positive.

_____

_____

_____

_____

_____

_____

_____

Parent Toolbox

When having a conversation with your teenager, are you aware of the positive and negative talk that they already use? Are you aware of the positive and negative words and phrases that you use when talking to them?

As a parent, every conversation you have with your child or young adult can have a massive impact on their internal self-belief and the way they handle inner changes to their emotions. This can lead to either positive or negative inner thoughts about their worthiness and value in life.

A great Strategy for improving conversation between you and your teenager is to have structured or agreed times when you sit together, perhaps over a coffee, and talk for 10 minutes to half an hour while both using 'awareness' of the conversation to help discover the words and phrases that could be turned into more positive thoughts and self-talk.

You can treat these sessions like skills-practise without the pressure of getting it right or wrong, but by learning together. You can even go as far as taking a lesson from each conversation, to focus on improving for the next conversation.

My son and I used to have these talks while out in the car if it was a journey of at least half-hour. It can also be on a walk, or over the phone if you don't live together.

Key Points

The skill of managing inner change will not only help to grow through these exercises and the understanding of positive change but also help you to carry these skills into the outside world and help you change your outlook on life for the better. This, in turn, will raise your coping strategies to help you cope better with future changes and challenges.

My son realised upon grasping this that he became stronger. He said *"I now know why steel is forged in the fire. The more you go through it, the tougher you get."*

He realised that there would be more challenges ahead, but he was ready to face them head-on.

OUTER CHANGE

This is when something happens to you, such as being spoken to rudely, falling off your pushbike and grazing your arm, being scared by a horror film or eating dodgy fish. Something or someone has had a negative effect on you, not through your own choice.

Outer change is a little different from inner change. Outer change is something we have less control over. The world is full of changes that seem like an infinitesimal equation of possibilities. This can be things that happened in society, in your family, with your friends, at school, at work, in politics, with your money and many other possibilities.

Outer change can happen to you at any time without warning. It can also be something you expect to happen that doesn't, such as a friend not turning up for dinner.

The seasons change, the weather changes, your body changes. This is different to the inner changes of your mind.

Your life changes all the time, as you grow from a baby to a toddler, child, teenager and eventually to an adult. You change throughout education, and as you progress from school to college and university. You may change from job to job throughout life, but most importantly, you will be able to embrace all these changes as progress.

The key point to understand here is that change is inevitable. You cannot prevent change from happening in your life, therefore learning to deal with change as effectively as possible is one of the most important skills you can learn in your life. The problem is this one most important skill of all, is not taught in school but you are expected to know and deal with it anyway as if it was natural to everyone.

Now you are learning this skill through the Mood Mentor Model; this does not have to be an unknown any further. You are holding the book that will help you learn about the world of change in a universal system that you can apply as a skill for life. This will put you leaps and bounds ahead of others who have not learned to master change.

Being able to utilise this skill in life will give you greater happiness, more resilience, and a better chance of getting a job, earning job promotions, or even getting good pay rises.

Mastering change will also help you to understand why other people are struggling to cope with change and make you invaluable to them when you have the answers instead. In fact, most jobs and businesses take the concept of mastering change for a niche topic such as managing someone's accounts, fixing their car, healing their body, painting their house, and many other skills.

In the same way, when you come across a change that you haven't learned to master and don't know where to begin, there are plenty of skilled people out there who can help you. This is what the world's economy is built on, solving people's problems.

Humankind has not woven the web of life.
We are but one thread within it.
Whatever we do to the web, we do to ourselves.
All things are bound together.
All things connect.
Native American wisdom.

The Diagram Explained

Just as in the Native American wisdom quote above, the orange outer circle of the emotional awareness diagram, binds all together. Notice how the diagram is like a simple form of this web with a centre That represents your mind, and outside that represents the world around you, and the four core emotions that are the threads within it binding it all together.

Just as the wisdom says, whatever you do to the web affects not only the world around you both positively and negatively but also the world within you. It affects your brain, your mind, your beliefs, your worth, and as a result, the actions that you give back to the outer world in return.

As you can see in the diagram, when you change through the outer change that encompasses all emotions, every change in life will affect you from the emotional state you are currently in, in either a positive or negative direction.

If you are already in a sad or angry state of mind when negative change happens, then negative change will feel more difficult to handle.

If you are currently feeling in a severely depressed state and positive change happens, it stands to reason that the positive changes may not instantly take you all the way to the top of the diagram of emotional awareness where happiness resides. It takes lots of small steps.

It will mean that moving up the diagram requires you to move through the emotions of anger or sadness, and face up to problems before you work through the emotions to find happiness again.

But realise that if this is you, then that yellow area at the top is there waiting for you. It really is the light at the end of the tunnel, and I will help you find your way there through this book.

Being at the bottom of this emotional cycle is why someone with clear depression finds it very difficult to smile at receiving a gift, or laugh when watching TV. They find it difficult to connect with purpose, or the ability to take positive action. Changes feel almost impossible at this level, and they feel lost. They find it hard to know what changes they need to address these dark emotions.

They may need the support of a parent, friend, or even a counsellor, to help them through the early changes, before being able to overcome the gravity that emotional change has forced upon them.

For people whose depression is the result of the outer change, this may be due to bullying, abuse at home, family separation, difficulty with learning, the grief of losing someone they love, loneliness and not having close friends, or many other reasons.

When you recognise that the changes you make towards the outside world also have the same two options of positive and negative actions, why would you choose the negative option? Rock bottom is rock bottom for a reason. Positive is the only way to go from here, or as they say – the only way is up.

Knowing this now, are you feeling a renewed sense of purpose for practising a positive mindset here on?

Are you ready to make changes for the better by taking outer actions that improve your life?

The Purpose Of Recognising What Changes Happen Around You

Just as with inner change, it is important to recognise what effect outer changes have on your life. It is also important to recognise what options you have to make changes, through actions that you take, or interactions that you have with other people.

Say, for example, you are preparing dinner and the knife slips. The knife cuts your finger, and now you are facing a change that you hadn't expected. It is essential to recognise that this change is one that needs urgent attention. As a result, you would normally fetch the first aid kit and apply a plaster to the cut.

You may also need to look at this change even further. Why did the knife slip and cut you? Is the knife blunt? Does it need sharpening?

Were you paying attention or being distracted by something outside the window?

It is important to recognise the changes that happened and caused the knife to slip in the first place. This is to help you prevent the same accident from happening again in the future.

On the other hand when positive change happens such as making your favourite dinner, and you add an extra ingredient today, if you enjoy the meal more than last time, then noting the changes to the recipe will help you improve it again in the future.

It is these acknowledgements of external change, both positive and negative, that create improvements, progress and growth, as well as prevention, solutions, strategies and remedies.

I hope you are truly starting to connect with the importance of change and why mastering change will help you master your own life.

EXERCISE 20:

LIST WORDS YOU MIGHT USE

Try writing a short Story or analogy, like the ones I had used so far, to describe a time when the outer change happened in your life - and what you did to overcome the change with brilliant results.

_____

_____

_____

_____

_____

Analogy

Today I saw a lovely little story on social media, about a wheat factory in the United States. It was in the days when families were so poor, that workers were taking home the used empty sacks to make clothes for their children.

The factory realised that the workers were recycling the sacks for children's clothes. They wanted to do something about this and looked at what choices they had.

In many business cultures, you might expect that they told the families off for taking the fabric. Instead, the factory did something incredibly amazing. They recognised the changes their workers were using to clothe their families at low cost.

Instead of stopping this or reprimanding their staff, the factory made a change that was unexpected. They understood the power of positive change and the ability they had to make life better for the people around them by creating change.

What the wheat factory did, was to change the sacks that they stored the wheat in.

They started using sacks made from flowery fabrics so that the workers could make prettier clothes for their children. The printing that was on the sacks for advertising was also made washable so that it would come out.

Explanation

This story demonstrates the true power of understanding outer change, over the inner change of anger and frustration. The owners of the factory understood their options. They understood that the sacks were a waste product and that allowing staff to recycle them would create a happier workforce without having to pay them extra money. They understood that by making this change, they were also changing the way people felt about them and their business.

In return, this would improve the business they received from their customers. It seems like a win, win all round, for the business owners, the workers, their children, and their customers. It had a positive impact on their local society.

....

You can't go back and change the beginning
But you can start where you are and changed the ending.
C.S. Lewis

....

When you can learn to manage change in this way, you hold a powerful mindset and a skill that will change other people's lives for the better as well as your own.

Example

Think about something in your life where it hasn't always gone as you would like. Is there anything you can do to change what has already happened? The chances are that the answer is no.

Can you now see that because things haven't always gone the way you wanted, it doesn't mean that from today onwards it will always be the same. *You* have options, *you* have choices, and *you* can change the way things happen from today onwards.

Whatever you do to make changes from here on, make sure they're positive both for you and other people. To create changes in your life that make other people's life worse off is not positive change, it is the equivalent to abuse, bullying, neglect of your behaviour, and being toxic towards other people.

The true power of change will always make everybody's lives better.

Keep reading to learn more about recognising the types of outer change that you can make for yourself. Always start with making changes for yourself before you begin making changes for other people. Even this will make the lives of people around you happier when you are happier in yourself.

Be aware that when you try to make changes that affect other people's lives while neglecting your own changes, this can appear to be judgmental, controlling, or needy, as if using their problems to avoid dealing with your own.

There is a saying that when on an aeroplane, always put your own oxygen mask on first before helping other people. The same applies in general to anything in life that can have an emotional impact on both of you and the people around you.

Focus on making changes for yourself first.

Think about how my life improved when my son started to change, yet he didn't change FOR me, he changed for himself.

EXERCISE 21:

YOUR OUTER CHANGES

Write about something in your life that you would like to change, where it is important to focus on yourself before you help anyone else.

_____

_____

_____

_____

_____

_____

This may be to your education, your fitness, how you keep your room tidy, spending less time gaming, or spending more time on your personal hygiene.

These are all changes that you can make for yourself that will also have a positive impact on the people around you by default.

Parent Toolbox

When talking to your teenager about changes, it helps to discuss change in terms of inner and outer just as we have looked at in this chapter. It is empowering to them to recognise the correlation between things happening around them and the way they feel. It is also empowering to them, to have a greater understanding of why change helps them to feel better, rather than simply feeling like change is a string of instructions, parents reel off every day.

This chapter about how to change is the beginning of problem-solving by recognising the difference between positive and negative change. It is a significant step in personal development and recognising the power that they have to make changes within themselves. However, clever making these changes may still be complicated for some to grasp in the early stages, and this is where your support in small steps, will significantly help them on their journey.

Rather than trying to solve all their problems for them, it is teaching and mentoring them through these changes that bring about the most effective transformation of all in emotional improvement and wellbeing. It is also the difference between *parenting* and *mentoring*.

It is when I stopped parenting and started mentoring my son that he always made the biggest progress of all times.

Being beside Matthew on his journey rather than pushing him through it, was is the most effective strategy I have ever used - and would like to think this book gives you the same confidence to walk beside your teenager - and help them understand that this journey is *their* journey and that you are beside them all the way should they need to ask you anything at all.

I highly recommend that anytime they do reach out to you for help, that you listen without any judgement, see their point of view, help them understand why they see it that way and help them learn to find a new way of looking at life in a more positive way so that they can take their own steps forward towards a better future.

Key Points

Now you understand a bit more about change, and that it happens around you and within you, every single day can be a day where you face change head-on and start to live a fuller life.

Change will happen no matter what, and some changes will need to be accepted for what they are, no matter how hard it seems.
Occasionally change becomes a real barrier to life, but I will cover that more in chapter three when we talk about root causes.

There are also many more changes that you have the power to initiate, and start to lift your mood through choice.

"The road to success is always under construction."

Lily Tomlin

CHAPTER 2: OPTIONS

A holistic approach to exploring changes in your life – Are you aware of the different options in which you could explore these?

Options are having a choice when something changes. Do you feel like your parents are constantly telling you how to live your life? Are you faced with so many options you feel lost?

If so, this may be their way of trying to help you cope with the changes of moving into adult life. They merely want to share their experience, but you know that life had also changed since they were teenagers. As a result, you become at loggerheads with each other but trust me, don't write them off yet.

Have you considered that your parents are trying to help you learn about change but do not know how else to explain it?

Instead, they say things like;

> "There's light at the end of the tunnel."
> "It's just a stepping stone."
> "You can get yourself through this."
> "Grow up and act your age."

It can feel overwhelming, but parents really do not know how else to help you, so cut them a little slack. Try and connect with them about the book if you can.

The one thing your parents do understand is that the light does exist at the end of the tunnel when you come out of depression and reconnect with life. What they don't know is what the map of 'your' tunnel looks like. They don't know how to shine the torch for you to find the way. But I do, and I did it for my son.

Matthew found his way to the lighter side of life and said it felt like his brain had become unchained. Hence, he chose the title of the book for me.

This book can help bring you and your parents back in line with each other by understanding *your* options through the following part of the Mood Mentor Model and why they were trying to share what *they* see as your options, to help you.

Analogy

> When starting to help my son on his personal development journey, I began to realise the patterns in why his emotions were changing. As I learned about his changes and reflected on my own, I also found my own mind-expanding and recognising these same patterns across the globe. These patterns were consistent to everyone regarding of age race religion, which football team they support, their mental well-being, their job, and much more. The key point was that the patterns applied in exactly the same way to everyone.
>
> It may appear that if you were to write a book about problem-solving, that you could not include every problem in the world. And this would be true but knowing that every problem fits within a universal pattern, helps you to break each problem down to an understandable starting point.
>
> When you recognise that the same patterns that cause problems are also the same as the patterns to finding happiness, your new-found knowledge gives

you a leading edge on taking control of your life, your skillset, your positive thinking, your own problem-solving skills, and the ability to live life to the full.

There are millions of things that can change in your life, yet they can all be broken down into just five categories.

By learning what these categories are, it gives you a clear starting point for identifying all the different things that are changing in your life, how they change your emotions, feelings and beliefs, and how you can create your own challenges out of everything that happens for better or worse.

Knowing how to do this helped you break seemingly overwhelming situations, down into smaller, more manageable information, and enables you to deal with challenges one small step at a time.

You can also learn to appreciate and sustain good changes by creating lasting habits that help you grow continuously.

As you learn about each of the five categories of change, I would also like you to think about each change in terms of previous lessons in this book.

Try to link together the categories, with the previous lessons of...

- *The four Core Emotions*
- *Strengths and Weaknesses*
- *Positive and Negative Thoughts*
- *Inner Change and Outer Change*

I will set some exercises in each of the five changes, that will help you think of ways to link these.

When you can understand each concept in this book separately and then link the lessons together as you need, you can start breaking that chain that holds you back and makes you feel stressed, anxious, depressed, and leaving you feeling like there is no hope!

Let's get started on learning what each of the five change are so that you can begin recognising your barriers, challenges, and the options that you hold the power to make.

5 STEP MODEL FOR H.E.L.P.S.

In the whole world, there are millions of things that can change, yet they can all be broken down into five categories. Knowing this gives you a clear starting point for identifying your own challenges, and things that are changing in your life, for better or worse, so you can sustain good change, and challenge the negative changes.

HEALTH

Health is always the first of the challenges that you should check when feeling out of sorts.

Food: Some health problems are easy to miss, and just as easy to resolve. Many people find that when they are hungry, they get angry. I know I do.

This is a simple link between emotions and changes. What changed was they became hungry. This can easily be solved by having something to eat. If they don't eat and let the anger win, they may say something that hurts other people's feelings, or if they are angry, they may find it hard to concentrate on their work.

Then there's overeating. It becomes hard to concentrate because your body's energy is too busy trying to digest food, and you get tired or fall asleep, just like after a big meal and lots of sweet food at a celebration. At worst, it affects your weight, which then affects your self-confidence and ultimately, your physical health.

*Food is a **major** link between your emotions and health.*

Just as eating too little or too much can affect your emotions, another major factor is WHAT you eat. Eating healthy food leads to healthy emotions as well as a healthy body. However, working out for a healthy body but still eating junk food can still lead to an unhealthy mind.

Your brain and your body require a whole range of nutritional components to rebuild, replenish and re-energise your body. If you eat toast for breakfast, a cheese sandwich for lunch and a pizza for tea, it may seem like you've eaten different things, but the toast, bread and pizza base, are all largely the same thing – flour. It's not really a varied diet.

Imagine you ate porridge for breakfast, had a tin of soup for lunch, then fish and chips for tea, then it's a little more varied and slightly healthier, but there's still room for improvement.

When my son had moved out of home and resorted to living on pizza, chips, or not eating at all, his depression became *very severe*. I talked to him about his diet and how it affected his emotions. The next day he cooked up some rice, lightly fried some mushrooms, then warmed up some blue cheese with some cream to make a sauce, and put some freshly boiled broccoli on the side.

The day after eating this, he phoned me to tell me what he had cooked, and how much better he already felt for having eaten a healthy and tasty dinner. In addition to the food, the added emotion of having taken *action* to cook something healthy for himself made it even more effective.

Drink: Do you have a headache? Eyes dry or blurred? Feeling dizzy? It's worth checking your fluid intake before assuming you have something more traumatic.

You may have been having fluids, but if it's not quite enough fluids over a long time, it can lead to numerous health problems that appear more complicated than they are.

If you have not been drinking enough fluids for sports, the activity plus onset of headache, dizziness and muscle cramps, sweating, panting, and dry mouth is easy to associate with needing water.

If however, you have had low fluid intake over weeks or months, you can get dry, itchy skin, twitching and cramps, blurred vision, lack of sweating, body odours, fatigue, confusion, anger, anxiety, and much more.

Your body will live for a long time on little fluid, but there's a difference between staying alive and living healthily.

"If you feel generally unwell, always drink plenty of fluids, then see what symptoms you still have afterwards."

How do I know if I have drunk enough fluids?

That's a really great question, and there is a really easy way to tell how good your body's hydration level is. It's called your wee.

- If your wee is really dark like a rich apple juice or darker, and smelly, you are really dehydrated and should drink at least a couple of glasses of water.
- If your wee is yellow, you are still dehydrated and should drink at least a glass of water.
- If your wee is pale yellow, you are getting there but a glass of water, or at least half, should still be beneficial.
- If your wee is clear, or barely yellow, well done, you have been drinking plenty of fluids and taking care of yourself.

The clearer your wee, the less it will smell.

Water is also a good way of flushing out toxins if you've been on an unhealthy diet. It's a simple way to keep an eye on your health, every time you go to the bathroom.

No one will even know, just take a single second to be alert before you rush to flush.

If you let the dehydration continue, keep working, running, sunbathing in the heat, you become unable to function socially and start snapping at anyone who talks to you, or you run and hide in your room, blaming it on the headache instead of listening to what it was telling you. Your headache then gets worse; your social life falls apart, you just can't smile for anything, and all because of a glass of water.

It's obvious to see that being dehydrated because you didn't drink any fluids, can be corrected by drinking some water, or some juice, milk, or any drink to help rehydrate your body and your mind.

If you are old enough to drink alcohol, be very aware that alcohol may feel wet when you drink it, but it dehydrates your body even more and does nothing to cure a headache.

I tend to live on coffee, and sometimes caffeine-free teas, and I love freshly squeezed juice, but every time I drink alcohol, I feel so dehydrated I always want a glass of water afterwards rather than another drink. It's good to be aware of your body's needs.

How much do you take your health and fitness for granted?

Health is a massive category of change in so many ways in life. Your health can get better or worse, be impacted in an instant, or decline over a long time. *You* can care for your health, or *you* can neglect it. At the end of the day, you have so many options around health; this too can be overwhelming.

Health is a massive barrier for many people, while others make their living from it. Think of some of the problems your family face, and how they go about getting help.

Health is the biggest moneymaker in our economy. From diet plans to medication, plastic surgery, hospitals, specialist help and more. Your eyesight and hearing also come under health, as does a regular visit to the dentist.

This whole series of industries and more, are based on helping you make positive changes when your health has taken a negative turn. Some industries, such as fitness plans, gyms, yoga DVD's and supplements, are aimed at helping you prevent those negative changes, by maintaining a healthy lifestyle, to begin with.

Think of a time your parents said

- "Eat all your dinner."
- "Get our for a walk instead of reading comics."
- Or "Don't forget to brush your teeth".

It may have sounded like they were nagging, but in reality, they were trying to help you stay healthy, and prevent your health from deteriorating. They just didn't understand how to explain this in a way that would empower you to want to make those changes for yourself.

....

It is health that is real wealth and not pieces of gold and silver.
Mahatma Gandhi.

....

Looking At Health Changes

Imagine having a day sick and losing a day's pay or missing an important exam. Imagine having a disability that has a massive impact on achieving what others see as normal daily tasks, like getting dressed.

If you are sick, it is difficult to earn money. Money pays for medicine when you are sick, or it pays for your fillings when you haven't brushed your teeth. It helps pay for therapy if you have hurt yourself, or may just cost a little more to eat healthy food. Therefore most people think wealth is a top priority, or at least Earning enough to live on. But how can you earn money to live on if you do not look after your health?

Imagine now, which is more important – Health or Wealth. If you had been asked this before starting to read Brain Unchained, would your answer have been Wealth?

Health is also a major entertainment factor, such as dancing and sports, just as two examples of many. Is there anything you do for entertainment that benefits your health and fitness? Do you like skateboarding? Running? Horse riding? Cycling? Or something else entirely like martial arts, climbing, or even running a paper round. If you already have a job, how important is your health to performing your role in that job?

Many teenagers also struggle with their diet. From eating mainly junk food that offers little nutrition to overindulging on big portions, or under eating and suffering the effects have anorexia, bulimia, and other eating disorders.

All of the health changes that I have talked about so far; all have a strong connection between outer change and inner change. The better you feel on the outside, the better you feel on the inside. The worse you feel, the more it impacts your emotions on the inside.

When you understand the correlation between your health and all the outer actions that you take and the way it makes you feel on the inside, you can begin to reverse the process with positive thinking and work on feeling better from the inside so you can make better changes to your health on the outside.

When you learn to take control of your emotions around health, you also by default, learn to improve your wealth which also enhances your emotions even further.

Health can also be a strength. It can be knowledge, and it can be a skill. Think about someone who's health they consider a strength, so much that they study and learn enough to turn that strength into a skill like personal training and working in a gym, or learning about medicine to become a pharmacist, or learning about the body itself to become a doctor, nurse or one of many types of physical therapists.

Some people enjoy learning about food and cooking, yet again this can be a strength for someone who chooses to study food as a nutritionist, as opposed to baking cakes or serving junk food. You can start to see the pattern about the way positive health can be used as a starting step for a great career that helps other people to improve their health too.

Health also offers some of the biggest challenges, both positive and negative. Think about the thousands of people every year who choose to run a marathon. This goes beyond an everyday challenge and allows the person to set a goal with an *outstanding* challenge that they need to train for. The same could apply to swimming long distance, cycling from Land's End to John

O'Groats for charity, or choosing to join a weight-loss club with the aim of losing substantial amounts of body fat.

Each of these outstanding challenges will be faced with great difficulties that push mental barriers to the limit, but when each person has the right support in place to help them through those barriers, the most amazing transformations and achievements can then take place.

Inner And Outer Health

Just as mentioned about running a marathon, as much as it requires physical stamina, so it requires emotional stamina. Imagine trying to run a marathon if you allow your brain to constantly tell you that the distance is impossible. What will your chances be of ever reaching the finishing line?

Now imagine spending time every day when you wake up, telling your brain through affirmations and positive quotes, that this is your mission. That you will succeed. That today you will run further than yesterday. That the pain is growth, and growth only happens through the pain. Can you now imagine reaching that finishing line more easily with those positive thoughts in your head, than with the negative thoughts?

Sometimes your health will feel more like a barrier than a challenge. These are times you will need to apply some logic to work out what is happening with your health.

There are times when we all feel under the weather and don't know what the cause is. These are times when you are most likely to call a doctor and ask for an expert opinion, but there are many other times when you can learn to take more care of your own health and make your own changes for the better.

Sometimes all you need is a little TLC. It's always nice to have someone look after you when you feel under the weather, but you can also do some things to look after yourself as well, such as getting a hot water bottle, getting out for fresh air, eating healthy food, or sticking your own plaster on for minor injuries.

EXERCISE 22:

WHAT ARE YOUR HEALTH BARRIERS?

What health do you face, and what challenges will you set yourself?

_____

_____

_____

_____

Think about the answers relating to the following lesson's you've already covered…

Strengths:
What are your health strengths?

_____

_____

_____

_____

What does this help you achieve?

_____

_____

_____

_____

Weaknesses:
What would you like to improve about your health?

_____

_____

_____

_____

How can you make these improvements?

_____

_____

_____

_____

Positives:
What positive emotions do you have about your health?

_____

_____

_____

_____

What can you do to maintain this?

_____

_____

_____

Negatives:
What negative emotions do you have about your health?

_____

_____

_____

_____

What affirmations could you use to improve your emotions
around this?

_____

_____

_____

_____

Inner change:
What inner changes, do you need to make for your health?

_____

_____

_____

_____

Do you need any help with these changes?

_____

_____

_____

Outer change:
What outer changes could you make for your health?

_____

_____

_____

_____

How can you turn these into Positive Challenges?

_____

_____

_____

_____

If you find these questions are difficult to answer, try writing your own version in a separate notebook.

Analogy

Back in the days of Caveman Dan, he also would have faced many health challenges. His priority would be nutrition and finding food. His challenge would be gathering and hunting. He would also need to stay fit and healthy so he could hike long distances and run to hunt down his food.

Dan would need to be positive about his skills to use a spear while being motivated to keep going during the hunt so that he came home with a meal for his family.

Dan would have also needed knowledge of what to do when they were unwell, or maybe the mother of the family would have learned - like studying medicine today – about the healing benefits of herbs, berries, tree bark, and using plants like moss to stem minor wounds and prevent them from becoming infected.

Dan and his family would also have learned how to eat differently for the seasons to ensure winter survival, which is something we don't think about as much today.

Whatever happened, Dan had learned to master changes in seasons to change the skills he needed, to keep his and his family's health as well as possible.

....

Take care of your body. It's the only place you have to live.
Jim Rohn

....

This quote is so true. When your body falls apart, and ultimately breaks and gives up trying – where else will you live? Surely with that knowledge, you will want to take care of your body sooner rather than later. Keep your literal home alive – your body - and you will live a happier life no matter what house you live in.

Setting Health Goals

Think about Caveman Dan out hunting, and how that translates into sports today. As a modern civilisation, we don't hunt for our food; we shop for it. This takes away – especially for a man of the house – the ability to go through the emotional cycle associated with hunting.

I know some people do still hunt, but it is frowned upon today in most societies as being an unnecessary sport. Many more people don't take part in any sports at all and find that their health deteriorates all too soon in life. For you, now is the perfect time to start taking care of your health to the best of your ability.

Remember we talked about all inner and outer change being connected? Hunting is an outer need that forces inner changes to the emotional cycle. Dan would have worked through those emotions as part of the hunt, but how do you overcome this basic emotional need today?

Instead of hunting, many people approach the need for emotional release and positive inner change by playing football. They throw a ball in a field, then they all set goals and work as a motivated team to hunt the ball and get it into the goal before the other team can steal it. Then they all have a meal together in the clubhouse.

Can you see how the ritual is similar, but without actually chasing an animal?

Not everyone likes football, but the same feelings of emotional release can be found through running – just as Dan chased his prey. Archery – just as he would throw a spear, and other sports that use the same physical skills that caveman Dan would have used 10,000 years ago.

When you understand that no much how much our society, technology, science and medicines have changed since caveman days, that your emotions haven't changed at all from the emotions Dan would have felt - you can begin to apply the lessons from Dan to living a life today that is equally as fulfilling to inner and outer health but with many more benefits than Dan had.

EXERCISE 23:

SETTING A NEW HEALTH CHALLENGE

I know we've already done one exercise on health, but I would like you to think about one single change that you can make to your health through a single positive challenge.

_____

_____

_____

_____

Is your new challenge a short term goal, for example walking a mile a day for a week? Or are you setting a longer-term goal such as learning a new sport or training for a marathon?

_____

_____

_____

_____

Keep a log of your progress, your emotions, and things you find yourself saying both positive and negative, and focus on repeating the positive aspects of your challenge, so you can keep improving on them, growing in strength, and ultimately achieving your desired goal.

A health challenge may also be something like changing your diet. This might be cutting out certain foods like burgers and chips, or sugary foods and drinks. You might not even be overweight but finding it difficult to focus your attention on anything and struggling with depression.

Adding appropriate foods into your diet to improve your nutrition can also help your emotional well-being. As long as you are not allergic to nuts, it is said to be good for mental health to eat a small handful of cashew nuts daily to lift your mood.

Vitamin D is also another factor of health that you could be lacking if you have not spent much time outdoors. Lack of vitamin D is proven to have a detrimental effect on mental health. Simply taking a tablet a day to raise your levels can be the start of helping yourself out of that depression.

On one occasion, I bought Matthew a bottle of vitamin tablets and labelled them 'Happy Pills' to make taking them fun.

If necessary, see your doctor for a blood test to cheque your levels, or cheque with the pharmacist on the recommended dose for your age, weight and lifestyle.

Parent Toolbox

Helping your teenager with health challenges may also require additional research, especially around hormonal changes, if they have any additional health challenges that need to be taken into consideration or disabilities. Any personality disorder may also affect the type of challenge they set and the support they need to achieve it.

Even with personality disorders and disability's, outstanding goals are achievable. It may help to do specific research around their challenges and find inspiration from other people who have challenged themselves through similar difficulties to achieve success.

Key Points

There are so many health changes that can affect your health, your wellbeing, problem-solving skills, and your possible career options that I could write a dozen books or more just about this section.

Instead, I hope that you have found a small spark to start making better changes to your health, or continuing the good work. Know your strengths. If doing any necessary research about health challenges for illness, disability, nutritional or dietary changes, to something else entirely, be careful not to focus too much on generic voice-over content on videos or puffed up advertising on blogs.

Instead, look for specialist advice. Join a gym, see a doctor, contact a local help group. Use the power of people and connect with *real* people who do know the answers that you don't know.

EMOTIONAL

Have you ever heard anyone talk about life being like a roller coaster, full of ups and downs, twists and turns and sometimes loop the loops?

The whole point of writing this book was about understanding all the challenges, and all the changes you can make to overcome emotional barriers. I've been asked on numerous occasions why I would need a separate category for emotions on their own. Surely if everything else in this book resolves emotions, they can't be a barrier on their own. Or can they?

Again I have thought and thought and thought about this topic, trying hard to find a reason to take this section out on the back of other people's comments, but always find a reason to leave it in.

For some people, this roller coaster isn't a barrier but a ride that they enjoy being on over and over again even when the ride gets bumpy. If you are like me and don't like roller coasters in real life, the chances are that you find it difficult to overcome certain emotions, to embrace life fully and make progress.

This is when emotions become a barrier. That moment when you are facing the roller coaster from the platform, knowing there's no turning back because the queue behind is blocking the entrance you just came through, and knowing you don't want to get on that ride.

What do you do?

This category, therefore, remains strong because many people face fears, phobias, stress, anxiety, panic attacks, and other emotional barriers that hold them back in life. These are real challenges that cause chemical changes in the body. Just like the Health category, these changes have an effect on your wellbeing, both physically and emotionally. Eventually, extreme fear can make you become sick.

Some fears can simply be accepted. For example, I have a fear of snakes, but it's not something I need to address, to cope with everyday life. If you wanted to be a vet or zookeeper and had a fear of snakes, you may have to look at ways to overcome your fears.

This does not mean throwing away all caution but stripping back all those *irrational* thoughts by learning about how to handle snakes, until *caution* is the helpful emotion brought to the front of your mind, to protect you in a positive way.

Looking At Emotional Changes

Emotions changed because something else changed. I keep reminding you this because it should always the first question.... **What changed?**

In this category, it is your thoughts that are changing and controlling your emotions, but your emotions don't know the difference between what you are thinking – such as snakes – or what you see – a real
snake.

This is the moment that your emotions go into overdrive. Just as we talked about emotions changing - your emotions treat this moment as 'fear'. Fear means danger in your mind, and it wants to change naturally, *so you can find a safe way out.*

Back to the rollercoaster. As a result, you would find yourself at this moment looking at every possible alternative, realistic or not, to see if there is a way of avoiding getting into that carriage. You will probably consider running back through the crowds (flight – blue) and shoving everyone out of the way but realise that shame is another fear, and you don't want them to see you in this state either.

So, you take a deep breath and think again. You think about running for the exit (Action – Red) but realise you have to go through the carriage to reach the opposite platform. How convenient for them! You think about just staying where you are and realise that's not going to achieve anything other than remaining stuck in this awful situation (No hope – black)

Your mind eventually runs out of *emotional options* and gets STUCK, not knowing which emotion to turn to next. You need to connect with an external change, but you HAVE to go through one of the four colours, and happy isn't happening!

You feel like that rabbit in headlights, torn between fight and flight. It may feel like the film Matrix - choosing the red pill or blue pill. Or the conundrum between two doors. One leads to escape, the other to – oh yes – a rollercoaster ride of emotions. The only option missing is the happy one (Freedom and joy – Yellow).

For someone who has no fear of rollercoasters, that yellow window of opportunity is the obvious one. They jump in, strap down and wait for the ride to begin. But that's not you. You have an emotional barrier, but why?

Inner And Outer Causes For Emotional Change

Several reasons can cause emotional barriers. Let's look at just a few examples:

Experience: Maybe like me, you fell down the stairs when young and hated the sensation of falling – primarily if you associate it with the pain that occurred when landing. Yes, my head hit the door at the bottom, and it hurt. That leads to the sensory fear of anything that feels like you are out of control such as funfair rides, flying and of course roller coasters.

My daughter also did this, but she tried to reach the light switch by standing in her dolls-pram and literally rode the stairs down. She still hates roller coasters too, but because she came down in the dark, she also hates being blindfolded.

Inherited: Fear may also be about many things that are not associated with pain. Spiders are a common fear that is passed on from one generation to the next. We learn fear from our parents.

Knowledge: This is like spiders but usually because adults teach you not to go near wasps - they sting, You are taught fear, to protect you. If you have an allergy to stings, this can enhance the fear even more because you *know* what the consequences can be.

Some fear may be from hearing stories, such as a fear of ghosts after storytime around the campfire. It may be a fear of dark from seeing the news and how people get hurt or start riots late at night. It might be a fear of meeting a new teacher because someone told you she was horrid and shouts.

Unknown: Fear of the unknown might affect you more if you have a hospital appointment for a scan or an operation. You don't know what they are going to do or what it will feel like – and that can be scary too. That is why hospitals try to give out leaflets with the appointment letters, to tell you what to expect. Some people then read this and have a fear of the knowledge instead, but at least it's not unknown anymore.

There are thousands of reasons why fear, stress, anxiety, panic and other internal emotions can get in the way of living life happily.

For most people, the fear of spiders is only on seeing one. The fear of flying is only relevant when going on holiday, or the fear of pain is only when facing a hospital appointment.

But what if that fear is more prominent. What if you are afraid of something even when it is not there, or you are not facing the challenge? How do you go about reducing that fear?

EXERCISE 24:

WHAT ARE YOUR EMOTIONAL BARRIERS?

What are the things in your life that cause you to experience fear, stress, anxiety or depression? Write them all down if there are more than one, and write the core emotion beside them along with any other notes that link back to earlier chapters...

_____

_____

_____

_____

Think about the answers relating to the following lesson's you've already covered...

Strengths:
What are your emotional strengths?

_____

_____

_____

_____

What does this help you achieve?

_____

_____

_____

_____

Weaknesses:
What would you like to improve about your emotional barriers?

_____

_____

_____

_____

How can you make these improvements?

_____

_____

_____

Positives:

What positive emotions do you have about your emotional barriers?

_____

_____

_____

_____

What can you do to maintain this?

_____

_____

_____

Negatives:

What negative emotions do you have about your emotional barriers?

_____

_____

_____

What affirmations could you use to improve your emotions around this?

_____

_____

_____

_____

Inner change:
What inner changes do you need to make for your emotional barriers?

_____

_____

_____

_____

Do you need any help with these changes?

_____

_____

_____

Outer change:
What outer changes could you make for your emotional barriers?

_____

_____

_____

_____

How can you turn these into positive challenges?

_____

_____

_____

_____

If you find these questions are difficult to answer, try writing your own version in a separate notebook.

Story

For many years, I feared motorbikes. I had a moped when I was 18 and fell off it three times in three months on ice and snow. I hurt my neck and shoulder a little, but I was ok. The bike needed more repair than I did.

The second time, I can still remember sliding along the road on my back in the snow, watching the stars wobble as the recent snow brought me to a stop. This fall happened because the weather was SO cold that my throttle had frozen and I couldn't slow the bike to take my exit. The bike actually sped up instead!

Now the thought of anything going faster than the 15 miles an hour crash, or the 30 miles an hour that the bike would go downhill, only filled me with more fear. What would happen if I was going faster and then crashed?

For many years this was not an issue because I had a car. I was proud that I was safer on four wheels than two and took great care to drive sensibly without testing the theory of crashing again. Well almost. Twice people ran into me while I was stationary.

When I was 48, my husband bought a motorbike and took his test. I was afraid he would crash. It was a 125cc, and he loved it, but I was afraid – for him. Then he took another test and got a 500cc bike. He wanted me to get on the back.

NO WAY!!!!!!!

He kept asking. I kept listening but saying no. At the same time, he was learning not just to ride the bike, but was watching YouTube videos on crashes, talking about why each one happened and what the rider could have done to avoid it. He was also watching videos on the right things to do, from people who taught safer riding. He discussed all of these with me and was proving to be very sensible about it all.

Because he was making such an effort to improve his knowledge, and every time going out to test the safer theories, coming home with delighted emotions of success – I finally agreed – because I was beginning to trust him – to get on the bike.

Here we go – suited, booted and skid lid on, I am 48 years old and shaking like a kid as we took the slow and daring ride of eight miles to visit our daughter. I held on so tight my arms hurt, but he was respectful of my fear and rode according to my feelings, not his.

As we left our daughters, at the end of her road, we were about to turn left when a car came flying around the corner. He applied the wrong break, the bike dipped at the front, he stuck his left leg out a little wide, the road cambered steeply, and he lost his footing.

I was promptly jumping off the pillion seat rather than falling because I 'knew' the risk of getting my leg trapped. I then turned to help him stop the bike, falling that last part of the way.

So – has my fear of bikes been made worse? No. Once again, I was falling off at less than 15 miles an hour – and in fact, we were at a standstill.

He apologised, explained what he had just learned

from the failure, and we got back on to go home. A bit like that roller coaster, I was faced with no other option than to get on and trust him, but somehow, I did trust him because of all the effort put into learning. By the way, this was all three months after taking his first test on the 125cc. He progressed quickly.

Two years later and a LOT of miles of riding around the UK, we packed one pannier each, and we spent ten days, travelling eight countries on a 1400cc motorbike, reaching as far as Italy. We spent three days crossing the Austrian, Swiss and Italian Alps, on mountain passes with continuous runs of hairpin bends. We even found ourselves in a thunderstorm, 3500m above sea level and for the first time in my life, I watched lightning from cloud level, going down into the valleys, rather than looking up at it. Absolutely incredible! Even if we were extremely wet and cold.

I would never have achieved this if I hadn't looked at overcoming past experiences, learning knowledge from my husband and YouTube where other people shared their experiences, wearing the right gear, and gradually turn all the unknowns, into known facts - about riding skills, about the bike itself, about the journeys ahead, and about what to do in an emergency - so I could turn all this into new and successful experiences.

I still had elements of fear when on the bike, but I also chose to focus on the positive things. The scenery, the sensations, the communication between us, and unlike being a car passenger, switched off – I would be watching and feeling every move he and the bike made, so I would know how to ride pillion safely for both of us. We rode as a team, and I overcame my emotional barriers to enjoy some of the most amazing experiences in my life.

....

A Wiseman changes his mind; a fool never will.
Icelandic proverb

....

Imagine if I had never changed my mind about motorbikes, and the adventures I would have missed.

Equally, if a friend tells you a new teacher is horrid, be open to changing your mind – and making your own judgement. She might be the best teacher ever, but your friend heard it from someone who heard it from someone etc.

Setting Emotional Goals

Some fears are acceptable to a degree, such as a fear of heights prevents you from going places where you could fall, but some people like to challenge this and set goals to overcome their fears. They bungee from bridges, jump out of aeroplanes, climb mountains and other crazy stuff. That's all quite extreme but perfectly brilliant if you choose to set these goals and push your comfort zone.

On the other hand, meeting new people – teachers, managers, strangers, the staff at the local supermarket, can also be frightening for someone who is afraid of making small talk. Setting a goal to say hello and smile to one person a day might be equally as challenging as setting a goal to skydive.

Look at your fears and think how even a small challenge can help you to grow, the way I did through the motorbike experience.

If you find something stressful, look at goals to *destress* such as meditating and using positive self-talk.

If you are struggling with depression, maybe you need smaller goals to eat more fruit and veg, walk outside every day, and take more care of your personal hygiene or style up your wardrobe to make you feel better.

Whatever goals you set – make them manageable but push yourself just outside your comfort zone and see how much these small changes will make equal changes in your emotions.

EXERCISE 25:

WHAT IS YOUR NEW EMOTIONAL CHALLENGE?

Refer back to the list of challenges you wrote about at the start of the chapter and set one or two small goals to help you work with them.

_____

_____

_____

_____

If necessary, make a separate log or journal, or even a progress chart, and set a reward that will help you work towards achieving your goals. Maybe even do this with a family member's support, where _they_ treat you to something – _making it more rewarding._

Parent Toolbox

Helping teenagers become aware of emotional barriers may require talking about memories or using old photos to discover when the fear began. This should be a positive talk of discovery. It is important to hold back all judgement, and not to laugh at why they have these fears.

It is also good to refer to the points in this chapter to help them discover the type of fear – the four here are just examples – and talk about strategies that could help them reduce the fear.

Accept that (depending on the fear they have), sometimes a fear will never disappear entirely, but making it easier to live with is a huge accomplishment in itself.

Did you know that the biggest fear of all for a majority of people, is speaking in public? The funny thing is, no one ever told me as a child that speaking was a fear.

I love talking and even did a TEDx talk in 2017 - about tackling teenage depression!

Key Points

This chapter barely touches the surface of fear, anxiety and depression, but I hope you can recognise that when you have read the whole book, done all the exercises, made changes in your life, and resolved many different emotional challenges in your life…

…If you find you still have some emotional issues to deal with, that this is the chapter to come back to and see what emotional barriers are left to deal with.

Then is the time to think about getting outside help if those emotional barriers are impacting your daily life and stopping you from enjoying life to the full.

LOGICAL

Do you like doing puzzles? This could be crossword puzzles, jigsaw puzzles, building Lego, following wiring diagrams, and many other kinds of logical challenges.

Logical challenges are one of my favourite categories. I am a problem solver. I love puzzles, I love challenges, and as an administrator for many years, I earnt my wage fairly by solving problems within my job role. I was well known for being the go-to person when other people's logic failed.

I once spent two days in a trailer sorting engineering spare parts against a stock list, when Warehouse staff, engineers, and account-department staff had given up trying to match the items to the stock list. I matched around 200 electrical spare parts for wind turbines and finished with just 30 that didn't match the last 30 items on the list. These were items that had been picked and packed incorrectly, then arrived at the warehouse without being checked correctly.

I have used the same skills of puzzle-solving and logic to help my own son through chronic depression and being suicidal, to create the system in this book by mentally filing and organising emotions, challenges, and root causes into a system that will help you understand the power of change for your emotional cycle.

Logic is a skill itself, yet it covers many topics. Some people use logic to resolve medical problems and heal people. Some used logic in engineering, and mechanics to fix cars, wiring and electrical problems. Some design solutions, such as architecture or new inventions. Some use logic for dealing with finances and investments, managing business, studying sciences, or solving global issues through charities an environmental work. The list is endless.

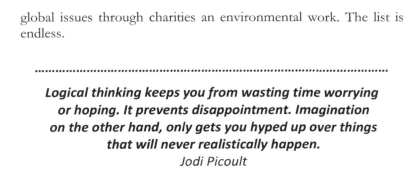

Logical thinking keeps you from wasting time worrying or hoping. It prevents disappointment. Imagination on the other hand, only gets you hyped up over things that will never realistically happen.
Jodi Picoult

This quote is really special for more than one reason. Not only is it so true that logic keeps you focused on positive thinking and seeking solutions that work, but I have also loved reading some of Jodi because novels, particularly "Change of heart". When my son was 15, he was about to publish a novel he had written at the age of 13, when he was asked to represent a local support group at a book launch in Norwich, Norfolk.

Jodi Picoult was the author and launching her latest book based on a character with Aspergers. My son also has Aspergers, and it was a special moment when he got to speak with Jodi Picoult and have his photograph taken with her while she signed a copy of her latest book for him.

Looking At Logical Changes

Logic is a real matter of fact subject and a complete counterpart to emotions. Logic becomes stronger with everything you learn and every experience you gain. Logic is one of the smartest skills you can work on. When something is broken, you either fix it yourself, or you find someone with the skills to do it for you. If we could apply the same logic to our emotions; the world would be a happier place.

If a door is locked, it needs a key. If someone is hurt, you call for help. If you drop something, you pick it up. When your clothes no longer fit because you've grown, you buy new clothes.

Logic is about recognising the connection between every action and reaction. It's about recognising the ins and outs, the ups and downs, and the fails and successes of everyday life that *you* can easily reverse or challenge through the knowledge you already know.

Logic is also about the language connecting clues with answers such as crossword puzzles, riddles, anagrams, word searches, and other games and puzzles. These are great at training your brain and keeping it fit and healthy in the same way you would use the gym or weights or running, to keep your body fit and healthy.

As a child, your early logic would be tested by asking you to fit shapes into holes such as triangles squares and circles. As an adult, you might have to match a key to a door from the bunch that you keep in your pocket. As a job, you may have to learn many skills that are based around logic; however, there are many times in life when logic fails you too.

Inner And Outer Causes For Logical Change

How many times have you heard someone say *"This doesn't work"?* Then someone tries to help them find out why it's not working. Half an hour later they're still both scratching their heads when you walk up and switched the plug on for them. These are the times when failed logic can be really funny in hindsight.

Other times logic can be more stressful when it fails you. Imagine you have missed the bus home and your first logical thought would be to call for help, but your phone has run out of credit. What would you do now?

This is a challenge my son once had, and he walked over a mile in bad weather, till he found a shop in a small village, where he borrowed their phone to call me. He had forgotten that he could call the operator and ask for the charges to be reversed, saving himself a long, cold walk.

Better still the most logical thing to do would be to keep an eye on his credit level and never let it run out.

Logic is also a barrier when you are struggling with a challenge, getting stressed over it, trying the same things over and over without success. Instead, you could be searching online or watching videos for the right way to do it or asking somebody else if they know an easier way to do it. Letting pride get in the way of asking for help can also get in the way of learning new logic and overcoming problems. Pride prevents progress!

EXERCISE 26:

WHAT ARE YOUR LOGICAL BARRIERS?

Try thinking of some logical solutions that you would use for some of the challenges you listed earlier. Also, think about challenges where you are missing information and could ask other people to share their logic.

_____

_____

_____

Think about the answers relating to the following lesson's you've already covered…

Strengths:
What are your logical strengths?

_____

_____

_____

_____

What does this help you achieve?

_____

_____

_____

_____

Weaknesses:
What would you like to improve about your logical barriers?

_____

_____

_____

_____

How can you make these improvements?

_____

_____

_____

_____

Positives:
What positive emotions do you have about your logical barriers?

_____

_____

_____

What can you do to maintain this?

_____

_____

_____

Negatives:
What negative emotions do you have about your logical barriers?

_____

_____

_____

_____

What affirmations could you use to improve your emotions around this?

_____

_____

_____

_____

Inner change:
What inner changes, do you need to make for your logical barriers?

_____

_____

_____

Do you need any help with these changes?

_____

_____

_____

Outer change:
What outer changes could you make for your logical barriers?

_____

_____

_____

_____

How can you turn these into positive challenges?

_____

_____

_____

_____

If you find these questions are difficult to answer, try writing your own version in a separate notebook.

Story

> The brother of my third great grandfather was a steamship captain in the 1800s. At the age of 24, he had already been working at sea for 10 years and had experience working on vessels that were cable laying in the China sea.

He was already a captain because of his hard work and dedication, and the vessel he was working on was due to begin another cable laying mission when the project-manager was suddenly taken ill the day the mission was due to start. The captain had a strong sense of logic and knew the job well enough from his earlier missions.

Rather than cancel the mission and lose thousands of pounds of work, he said that he would project manage the mission as well as captain the vessel. He not only completed the mission successfully but did so under budget and before the deadline.

Can you even begin to imagine the amount of logic he had, to achieve that at such a young age? Do you think he would have succeeded if he hadn't watched and learned from other people, and asked lots of questions?

Learning new skills is not only good for your career and your brain but also your self-worth, your emotional wellbeing, and the value you hold to others. It gives you a great sense of purpose when you can solve problems that other people need help with.

Remember I said I was an administrator? I worked with managers and engineers, but every one of them had their own logical skills, and they were all highly intelligent, university-trained people. I didn't even go to college, yet my sense of logic still held strong.

One logical challenge that always made me laugh was giving any engineer or I.T. technician a comb-binder, for binding documents together. It rarely took longer than twenty-second for them to give up trying and on some occasions, even throw the plastic combs in frustration!

I became so valued in the company for my logic, that

when they no longer had a facilities manager, rather than hire another, the power plant manager took the title (I didn't have the qualification) and mentored me. I ran the role as a Facilities Coordinator, managing 30 contracts to maintain the office and warehouse buildings and services.

In addition, to just running facilities for eighteen months, I used my admin skills to align the role with the offshore planning department, so they could eventually blend the role into their work and manage all the permits and work releases. All while trying to help my son move forward as he recovered from suicidal depression - and plan my TEDx talk - while retraining in Adult Education and Public Speaking. Phew!

Needless to say, even I suffered burnout after that - but I did it, and I grew from it.

I did it all because I treated every new challenge as a puzzle that I was determined to solve. Sometimes I failed, but when I failed, I learned more. When I learned more, I achieved more.

School and education systems put a great sense of importance on logic, although they don't always talk about it in the literal sense. They ensure that you put a focus on English maths and Sciences because these are the most logical subjects that exist.

These subjects cross-link with other subjects such as history, arts and crafts, music, woodwork, cooking, sports, and pretty much anything you can imagine.

Think about a topic you like learning about, and how you can improve your logic in this area. This may even be hairdressing and learning about the chemicals of hair dye, or personal training and the logic of movement for the body. It could be baking and how to help the environment through better recipes, or to write music with the logic of psychology, for motivation and inspirational listening. The combinations are endless.

....

Your whole life is solving puzzles. If you are curious, you will find puzzles around you. If you are determined, you will solve them.
Erno Rubik

....

If there's one man who has mastered the art of creating and solving puzzles based on logic, it's Erno Rubik. The man famous for inventing the frustratingly addictive Rubik's Cube. The logic it takes to solve the cube is incredible and way beyond me. Have you tried it? It's the same reason why I am writing for you now.

Setting Logical Goals

Think about how you can set goals to improve logic in your own life. This could be about better savings, or ways to complete homework more easily by following a system to write your essays like the systems in each chapter of this book.

Also, notice how logic links into the other four challenges and will be a very strong ally in Chapter three.

Use your imagination to set goals for learning new logic that link with the other categories in this chapter. This H.E.L.P.S. link the learning together in a logical way – pardon the pun. Here are some questions to help you think....

EXERCISE 27:

WHAT IS YOUR NEW LOGICAL CHALLENGE?

To start using this system to think about making yourself questions....power to growth!

What do you need to learn?
Who can you ask or learn from?
What different ways are there to learn?
What books do you have or could get to help you?
How can you practice?
Can you join a group or club (even online) to share learning?
Is it something you can use in a job?
If so, will it look good on your C.V.?
Do other people value you for your personal brand of logic?

Parent Toolbox

One of the most powerful lessons I learned about helping my son through depression was to stop mothering and start mentoring. This is particularly relevant to helping anyone grow their logical skills, the way in my managers mentored me to learn new skills at work.

Take time to talk through challenges where logic has both failed and succeeded and be sure to discuss the growth of success. Clearly outline the lessons learned from failure that leads to further growth in the future and the importance of embracing failure as part of the lesson.

Key Points

Logic is its own form of intelligence and can exist separately from higher education. Even the most intelligent of people, can often find themselves stuck when they face a new challenge for the first time, and struggle to apply the logic to overcome it.

Be aware of your logic as much as your emotions, taking note of where your logic is strong, and when to ask for help.

As a bonus quote, a friend recently told me, *("If you're sure of everything and nothing works, then something you've done sure must be wrong.")*

PHYSICAL

P hysical changes create some of the greatest barriers, challenges, and breakthrough moments of life.

Having an object in the way of a fire exit is a barrier that could cost lives. Changing this by keeping the doorway clear and setting regulations, ensures safety comes first, and lives are saved. It is through failure and past experiences that sadly, this lesson has been learned all too often the hard way because people fail to make the necessary changes for keeping safe today.

Health and Safety is a major subject on its own. There are so many regulations about fire safety, storing chemicals, wearing protective gear, using ladders or working at height, and much more, that everyone should be able to work perfectly safely.

When you apply the previous category of logic, combined with the regulations of physical challenges to ensure the safety of everyone in the workplace, it is a powerful tool. Many people make successful careers out are combining their logic and knowledge of safety, to help businesses stay within the guidelines and protect their workers and customers.

The government can also impose major fines for breaking these regulations. This is why it is important to become comfortable with the concept of barriers and their importance to both internal and external changes, to ensure everyone stays both safe – and happy.

Schools, colleges and universities are also classed as businesses which is why teachers would always tell you to wear your goggles in science, not running the corridor, walk on the left, don't push and shove. Other rules that sounded like nagging and control.

They were just trying to keep you all safe to prevent anyone from getting hurt.

Physical changes to your body can also be a major barrier to achieving everyday things. If, for example, you have broken your arm or leg, something like climbing stairs, brushing teeth or playing sports, all change because of the change to your body physically. When your body heals, and these painful changes change back to well-being, with healed bones, and muscles realigned through physiotherapy, your challenges naturally changes back. Physical barriers are a major part of army training through assault courses. Barriers are used to keep you out of dangerous areas and often have warning signs attached. Barriers help keep crowds organised by using lines of rope, especially going through customs at the airport. All these barriers Are put in place to keep you safe, but also because the outcomes of not having these barriers can be emotionally challenging.

Imagine going through customs at the airport without the ropes? Will the line of people be as orderly, organised and calm if everyone was pushing and shoving from all angles to get through a single customs checkout? What if telecoms didn't put barriers around there work holes, and simply let people fall in? Can you imagine the uproar or the emotions of the people who would get hurt?

So as you can see, physical changes can not only create a barrier in daily life, but barriers can also be used physically to improve everyday life.

The one barrier that I want you never to encounter in your life (if you haven't already) is the barrier of being behind bars. Use this book to help you understand all barriers, not just physical ones, to ensure that you live the best life possible and avoid the pitfalls that are all too often found through struggling with stress, anxiety and depression.

Finally, think about your bedroom door as a barrier, the purposes that this barrier holds for you. Think how it acts as a visual barrier to give you privacy, a physical barrier for holding in heat, a security barrier by deterring other family from walking into your room or taking stuff if the door is locked. This how it also becomes an emotional barrier that gives you a sense of safety when you are in your room and a social barrier when you close it to keep people out, or to have private conversations behind a closed door. The door itself is still a physical barrier made of wood, but it holds much more value than just plugging the door frame to your room.

....

Where loser saw barriers, the winner saw hurdles.
Robert Breault

....

....

A moment of anger can destroy a lifetime of work, whereas a moment of love can break barriers that took a lifetime to build.
Leon Brown

....

When reading these quotes, can you now see them with a whole new value than just words?

Looking At Physical Changes

As well as the barriers we have already talked about, think about the physical changes that happen in your health in other ways.

What happens if you put on way too much weight? How does that become a barrier to things like making friends? Getting a job? Playing sports? Doing everyday tasks? Or if you have excessive weight, even getting a seat at the cinema or on the bus.

What can you do to change around the new challenges? Do you have to sit in the aisle seats? Do you stop playing sports? Do you take jobs you hate doing? Do you find that all the changes you make are not ones you enjoy?

Instead, look at how can you make changes to other areas of your life to change your weight, such as moving a bit more, eating less, and even changing the types of food you eat. These are all physical changes.

Either way, you will make difficult changes.

More logical is if you physically break a bone, you go to the hospital where they put a physical cast around your leg, to protect it while it heals. Eventually, you do physical exercises to strengthen in again. Other times, they may need to operate and pin bones back together.

Physical changes also occur in your face over time. The more you laugh or frown, the more you change the muscles in your face, just as you would working out the rest of your body. Make time to be with friends and family who make you laugh – for the right reasons because these physical changes also occur emotionally.

Learn physical skills weather it's woodwork or hairdressing, typing, playing music, or becoming a famous footballer. Skills developed to expertise over time create a journey in you. The sky is the limit...

People love to see other people on a physical journey, whether it's watching tennis to see who reaches the cup-final or watching a single football match in hopes of that critical winning goal.

Watching ski-jumping is about praying that every jumper lands safely, while also secretly hoping for some exciting action when physics fails mid-air and tips them off balances sending them tumbling down the slopes.

These journeys are why T.V. makes a fortune out of reality shows and sticking a whole group of people in some remote place, and giving them challenges one after the other, to test their physical endurance. The winner may walk away with a prize, but the audience gets their enjoyment from watching that person go through their physical challenges and the transformation that happens emotionally at the same time.

Physical changes are also the basis for a great deal of humour, both in films, and video-fails online. People love those ones where skateboarders miss a physical barrier and crash to the pavement, or where they achieve success for sliding the board all the way along the rail, then trip going up a single step afterwards.

Inner And Outer Causes For Physical Change

Outer changes in our physical world are constant. They are part of your daily routine from brushing your teeth to eating, playing, getting to school, college or work, and every physical action your body takes. Every move you make is a change of position or changes where you sit, stand, or even the location completely. Other changes happen that block your way, or you bump into door frames, you trip upstairs, you cut your finger with a knife, or you even change the colour of your hair. These are all physical changes.

By being aware of which changes are physical, it helps us to separate these changes from the emotions that go with them. Cutting your finger may annoy you because continuing to work is more painful and difficult. Changing your hair colour may make you feel more powerful or cheerful. Tripping upstairs may make you feel embarrassed, or maybe you can just laugh it off. A door getting stuck when you are inside, may frighten you.

Every change has an emotional reaction, and now you can begin to be aware of your emotions and start making changes that you can, while maybe changing your emotions about some of the barriers you can't move, by being more positive. After all, it's hard work being angry about something you can't change, past, present or future.

EXERCISE 28:

WHAT ARE YOUR PHYSICAL BARRIERS?

What physical barriers do you encounter in your day-to-day life?

_____

_____

_____

_____

_____

_____

_____

_____

_____

Think about the answers relating to the following lesson's you've already covered...

Strengths:
What are your physical barrier strengths?

_____

_____

_____

_____

What does this help you achieve?

_____

_____

_____

_____

Weaknesses:
What would you like to improve about your physical barriers?

_____

_____

_____

_____

How can you make these improvements?

_____

_____

_____

Positives:

What positive emotions do you have about your physical barriers?

_____

_____

_____

_____

What can you do to maintain this?

_____

_____

_____

Negatives:

What negative emotions do you have about your physical barriers?

_____

_____

_____

_____

What affirmations could you use to improve your emotions around this?

_____

_____

_____

_____

Inner change:
What inner changes, do you need to make for your physical barriers?

_____

_____

_____

_____

Do you need any help with these changes?

_____

_____

_____

Outer change:
What outer changes could you make for your physical barriers?

_____

_____

_____

_____

How can you turn these into positive challenges?

_____

_____

_____

_____

If you find these questions are difficult to answer, try writing your own version in a separate notebook.

Changes are so incredibly powerful, that life would literally STOP if nothing ever changed. Money changes hands, time changes health, hugs and handshakes change your mood, and you can embrace all this to make changes for the better.

Analogy

The Grenfell Fire was a tragic and overnight change for many lives. It not only changed the lives of people within the fire, either losing a life or severely damaging their health, but even those involved without injury found their lives changed.

Either those escaping the fire unharmed but losing their home, or being involved within the rescue mission, will feel the emotional change from the physical trauma for many years to come. This includes family not at the scene but who lost loved ones, and the people involved in clearing up the scene, investigating the aftermath, and those looking to ensure the same never happens again.

One of the ways that health and safety can be dealt with on paper used to lie or use misleading information about the safety implementations put in place. For Grenfell towers, the information about the external tiles gave the impression the building was safe when, in reality, no action had been taken to replace the dangerous and flammable material that was used to clamp the building.

Lying about change, denying it, or covering it up, can itself create devastating changes further down the line. Be aware of your own integrity at all times and speaking the truth rather than covering up jobs that have not been done or speaking up about mistakes that have been made.

Long before Grenfell, I was working in an office, and on this day there was a large scale emergency training session for offshore workers. The operations room was filled with managers, coordinators, police and coast guards, while acting-press-reporters were constantly phoning for information on the incident, to apply realistic pressure to the training situation.

As the office administrator, I went to the kitchen to ensure the soup would be ready for everyone involved in training, only to encounter a strong and overpowering smell of gas. The young lady using the cooker had not ignited it properly and could not smell the gas herself. When I mentioned it, she went to ignite the cooker, and I had to stop her VERY quickly.

Realising we almost had a REAL emergency scenario right here in the building, I needed to report it! Especially as she couldn't distinguish the smell of gas – What if she did it again?

I knew how loud and busy the operations room was and that the health and safety manager was right in the middle of it all.

I asked myself; What was more important?

The pretend vessel offshore with an explosion in the hull and 150 people on board? Or the genuine gas leak in the kitchen?

I quickly wrote "Gas leak in the kitchen" on a stick-it-note, walked straight into the room and handed it to the manager. Initially, he laughed, thinking it was part of the training, but I said: "This is real." He instantly followed me to the kitchen to ensure everything was safe and find out why the gas hadn't ignited, to begin with when turning on the hob.

A week later, the same happened again with the same member of staff turning on the gas and not igniting the flame. Again I reported it.

By the following week, the managers had removed the gas cooker and installed an electric cooker to ensure the safety of everyone in the building.

Imagine if I had not reported it at all!

What if I simply covered it up or lied about it, and the member of staff did it again, but this time ignited the stove after the gas had leaked to fill the kitchen? How many people could have been hurt or even killed?

Some changes in everyday life may seem meaningless, but understanding the power of change can make life incredibly meaningful all round.

....

Many of the physical barriers you face are really - emotional barriers that you can overcome with a positive mindset.

....

Setting Physical Goals

What physical goals would you like to set yourself? Are these sports? Craftsmanship? Skillsets? Or something in everyday life like managing your chores effectively?

Think about how you feel emotionally about any goals you set. How has this challenge made you feel in the past? How do you feel about it after reading this book? How would you like to feel about it in the future?

If the answer is *"I haven't thought about this before."* Then that's an amazing answer because now you *are* thinking about it. Awareness is the first and most important part of creating change. After all, how can you change something you are not aware of?

Also, plan out a timescale and rewards for any goals you set. Have a vision by drawing out where you want to be, or what you want to achieve.

Write down some positive affirmations that will help you keep your mindset on achieving the goals, whether it's getting that new job, working out at the gym, walking the dog more, or helping your mum around the house so you can then spend more quality time together afterwards.

EXERCISE 29:

WHAT IS YOUR NEW PHYSICAL CHALLENGE?

Write down at least one physical goal that you would like to achieve.

_____

_____

_____

Write down something that has been holding you back.

_____

_____

_____

Write down some changes you may need to make to help you make progress,

_____

_____

_____

Write down someone who can help keep you motivated.

_____

_____

_____

Write down some positive affirmations that will help you believe in yourself, specific to achieving this goal.

_____

_____

_____

Parent Toolbox

Understanding the correlation between physical and emotional barriers is a huge learning curve. There will be many occasions in the coming years where your teenager will encounter more and more new barriers and need more understanding of how to overcome them.

This chapter should help you and your teenager to recognise that no matter what challenges they face physically, there is always a way forward. Sometimes this needs creative solutions; sometimes, it requires following rules and regulations preset for a job task to ensure their safety. Sometimes they need to recognise the need to stop feeling frustrated and ask for help.

There will also be times that these barriers will be more personal and based around their own physical abilities, or their personal beliefs. These are times when it may be worth having a conversation about how that emotional barrier for their logical mentality could be affecting their ability to tackle a physical task.

Key Points

The world of physical barriers is bigger than the world itself, and for some people even beyond, such as those choosing space missions to reach the moon and beyond in hopes that one day when the world can no longer physically support us, we will have greater options and to succumb to the downfall of this planet we live on now.

Now when life throws physical challenges at you of any kind, my hope is that you can now feel empowered to look at the physical barrier with a logical approach as in the last category and face them with a positive mindset that treats your emotional cycle to a happy ending every time.

SOCIAL

Should a great friend tell you to change to make their life better? Or should they tell you what great changes you make, by being in their life as you are?

Social changes are the ones that bring us the biggest joy in life. They also cut the deepest and hurt the most, depending on the change that happens.

Finding a new best friend, or having your heart broken is like the ultimate ends of the social scale growing up and reaching teenage years, but then there is losing someone close through death or illness that hurts deepest of all. Families splitting up, domestic violence and child abuse are also extreme social pains that hurt for many years after the physical or verbal trauma have ended.

If you are struggling to overcome trauma, then it is important for you to get support, as well as reading this book.

Social challenges are often the most difficult to resolve because they require the attention, the beliefs and the energy from both parties, to ensure the barriers are overcome. All too often, friendships fall apart permanently. Families struggle to co-exist, or work colleagues are just like bigger versions of school kids, sharing gossip, evil glances, and leaving you out in the cold.

From very small, children make and break friends. They feel delighted at making new friends and already feeling the extreme pressure of not being liked, being bullied, being ignored, and struggling to make positive connections.

Children today feel the social requirements all too young, to dress-to-impress, to be cool or popular, to be seen as likeable, and to be expected to feel confident and comfortable speaking up when the reality is, there are many more things in life they should be focused on.

Surely children should like dressing to suit themselves, love themselves first, understand their own strengths and weaknesses, and be building their own inner confidence before even considering what other people think about them, or even worse, imposing their own misshaped beliefs and judgements onto others.

This early parental and peer pressure to fit into society, find friends, have fun at nursery and playschool, be popular at primary school and the cool kid at high school, is overbearing, unsupportive to progress, and distracting from the real lessons in life. To be the best versions of themselves first and not turn it into some kind of competition, pecking order or gang mentality.

Instead, all this pressure and resulting behaviour destroys friendships, creates biases and negative self-beliefs, destroying self-worth and creating long-lasting emotional barriers to growing self-confidence and self-worth. It creates issues with body-confidence leading to eating disorders, and eventually social pressure to try things they wouldn't try on their own, like smoking, drinking and drugs.

If this is what your life has been like so far, I am sorry for anything that has created these negative experiences in your life but STOP and think RIGHT NOW…

Why should the rest of my life be the same? How do I want my life to be?

Today is the day. Your day. Start by reading this chapter and begin making changes to your own understanding about the social challenges that have helped put you in the emotional place you are in now.

Whatever has happened in your life this far, it is absolutely possible to start making changes within yourself. No one can stop you doing that – except YOU.

Start by examining your own self-beliefs, biases, and negative thoughts that have held you back this far. Also look at how you use these to connect with family and friends, to see what positive changes you can make here too.

It is time to change YOU for the better – and you will be amazed at how quickly the people in your life change for the better too, and discover who will support and nurture you to even *greater heights* than you could imagine.

You will also find that those who don't deserve you and behave toxically towards you will automatically pull away. It may seem hurtful at times but embrace the freedom from their limiting beliefs and judgment, to be a better you. Maybe one day they will also find their true selves and re-connect, but for now, that is their journey, and you need to focus on yours.

You become the average of five people you spend the most time with.

Jim Rohn

When you think about the people you spend the most time with, also take time to think about the qualities of each one that you admire the colour and how that influences you as an individual. Make a list if it helps.

Looking At Social Changes

Social changes are a category on their own. They are also the barriers and solutions to many of your other challenges.

We've already talked about how friends can hold you back through self-beliefs and judgement, but there are also many things that a friend can do to make your life better. If you are hurt or upset, having a good friend can be a great comfort. Something has changed your emotions, and a great friend will be beside you to help you feel better again, or if you are hurt, they will help you find the support you need whether it's finding a first aider or calling an ambulance.

At home, it is usually your family who share these moments with you, including offering TLC (tender loving care) when you are feeling unwell.

Most people will find that their family are there for them no matter what, but at the same time, through the intention of helping you to grow by offering advice, it adds stress to meet up to expectations rather than setting your own expectations at a manageable level for you.

Social challenges come in the forms of arguments, laughter and taunting, distancing and refusing to talk, blackmail, or emotional manipulation to name but a few. Be aware that these emotional challenges that the other person is trying to impose on you are often because they don't know a better way to deal with whatever barrier it is that is coming between you. Many people try to overcome barriers by controlling them, rather than reaching around them to nurture the friendships between you.

Understanding this can help you to see things from the other persons point of view so that you can nurture them to bring down the barriers if possible. Just remember that it is not your responsibility to resolve their behaviour, only your own.

A big social challenge often witnessed between friends that causes fall out's is when one person tries to force help on the other, to make them change.
You cannot help somebody if they do not want to be helped. You cannot reason with someone who is in denial or refuses help. The same applies to yourself receiving help, in that people cannot help you with anything in life unless you are aware of what you want to change and are willing to receive their help. That is why the very first chapter of this book begins with awareness, to become aware of where your emotions are, but every part of this book is about building on that awareness.

Many people go through life stressing, moaning and whining about the small social interactions every single day, and gossiping about things other people did, or what happened on last night's soap opera, or how their teacher or supervisor spoke to them today. Still, it helps to learn to be more positive and focus on your self-worth first.

It is too easy to let these negative thoughts affect your survival-emotions in a big way when they are not about survival at all. In fact, these negative thoughts can stress you out without really thinking *why*.

- What did you say when your team didn't score that goal, or your friend forgot to meet with you?
- Could you have worded it more supportively of their failure?
- Would this have helped you feel less stressed too?
- Did you give any thought to their emotions?

Why would you add all that stress to yourself, and then complain more about being stressed? It becomes a bad habit that eventually drives people away. Maybe you know someone else like this? How does it make you feel when all they do is moan about everything?

It is natural to do this because the human brain is built for negative-bias and is still following the pattern of Caveman Dan's emotional cycle in an attempt to keep you safe, but now you know about it, why would you still do it? Now you know about the options you have to be more positive, will you keep working on it?

Pay attention to the thoughts you have and the things you say about all of your social interactions, whether it's people you meet, watching the news, your favourite soap, or the last song on the radio and what the presenter said about the singer. Be aware of how they all affect your emotions. If it's negative, be mindful of changing it for the better. If it's positive, look at nurturing it more.

After all, awareness is the most crucial first step to making change.

Inner And Outer Causes For Social Change

Some of the biggest changes between people that cause problems are cultural, religious, or about sports and politics – and even more so when they combine or are fueled by alcohol.

The media is also another fire to the world of social changes.

Look at the changes this year about wearing masks in public, black lives matter, supporting NHS staff, supporting people who are lonely, and those who are still doing great charity work.

What about the changes of being stuck in your room more, or seeing less of your friends, moving to college or university, or trying to attend an interview online instead of in person, or not being able to shake hands and trying to make a good impression at a distance.

Social media has also seen some incredible changes, with people moving business online instead of face-to-face, or holding zoom conferences instead of travelling the road or the globe.

For myself, I've faced massive social changes this year. I lost my marriage after 28 years, my house we had lived in for 20 years, and lost yet another job. I was then ill, then in lockdown before having to move twice. I haven't been able to see my parents, children or grandchildren as much either. I've had *the most stressful year going.*

All these social changes are painful, and I've suffered anxiety and panic attacks this year too.

Knowing about the emotional cycle doesn't stop me having these emotions, but it helped me to recognise what changes I *could make* for the better, and to recognise which emotions I was *struggling* to change when I couldn't fix things like my marriage. These are the times when I was able to ask for help and focus forwards by doing lots of positive things with **intention**.

Then as I find a new place to live, we get another lockdown. Rather than spend 28 days alone for the second lockdown, I chose to do Live video talks about mental health awareness, every night for the whole 28 days, connecting people with stories to share, with people who needed inspiration. It gave me the social interactions I needed and helped other people at the same time. I also decided to use this time to finally write this book to help you.

Then realised that at some point in the future this will all change again.

I had other options – just as this chapter explains. I could sit alone and cry because I had lost my marriage, my job and my home and was now living alone somewhere new, or I could get online and do something about it, that not only benefited me but other people too. It was a choice that's not for everyone, but what options do you have to make you feel more sociable?

I would also like to mention here some of the great work that many people online do to connect with others by sharing 'How to' videos, or inspirational stories of the challenges they have been through, or even the twins in America that decided to start listening to old songs from all kinds of genres and simply recording their reactions.

This not only connected them with viewers but connected viewers with the incredible music of times past, and the stories within the music can be inspirational too. It's all human connection.

In return, they earned a following that earned royalties, and eventually, they had an online interview, when Barack Obama dropped in on one of their live recordings to congratulate them. If you want to look them up...

TwinsTheNewTrend - on YouTube.

That's the power of social change when you apply your passion and share what you love.

Social change can also be a family falling apart or maybe a grandparent moving away. It can be someone in the family having a change of health, or a parent losing a job and worrying about money. These all have emotional impacts that affect the social dynamics of a family. Just the same a gaining a new job or meeting a parent's new boyfriend or girlfriend.

EXERCISE 30

WHAT ARE YOUR SOCIAL BARRIERS?

Whatever social challenges you face, there are two rules....

1. Be the best version of you possible.
2. Be thoughtful about the five top people you spend the most time with.

Think about the answers relating to the following lesson's you've already covered...

Strengths:
What are your social strengths?

_____

_____

_____

_____

What does this help you achieve?

_____

_____

_____

_____

Weaknesses:
What would you like to improve about your social barriers?

_____

_____

_____

_____

How can you make these improvements?

_____

_____

_____

_____

Positives:
What positive emotions do you have about your social barriers?

_____

_____

_____

What can you do to maintain this?

_____

_____

_____

Negatives:
What negative emotions do you have about your social barriers?

_____

_____

_____

_____

What affirmations could you use to improve your emotions around this?

_____

_____

_____

_____

Inner change:
What inner changes, do you need to make for your social barriers?

_____

_____

_____

Do you need any help with these changes?

_____

_____

_____

Outer change:
What outer changes could you make for your social barriers?

_____

_____

_____

_____

How can you turn these into positive challenges?

_____

_____

_____

_____

If you find these questions are difficult to answer, try writing your own version in a separate notebook.

BONUS EXERCISE 31:

YOUR SOCIAL CIRCLE

List the five people that you spend the most time with, at home, school, education, friends, or work.

_____

_____

_____

_____

_____

Now think about how people can influence you without being in your immediate contacts.

Who is your favourite actor?

_____

Who is your favourite musician?

_____

Who is your favourite author?

_____

Who is your favourite teacher/supervisor/manager?

_____

Is there someone else that is really special to you?

_____

Do you spend more time thinking about one of these people above, than someone in your top five? If so, why?

_____

_____

Now re-write your top five, using both lists to create one ideal list. Use the one where you actually meet and know the people around you, and the one where you learn, listen to and watch people you have never met.

_____

_____

_____

How different does your top five look now?

_____

_____

_____

You don't have to cut people out of your top five to adapt it; you just need to change focus on who you take influence FROM. You can adjust this list at any time by reading a different book, finding a mentor online to follow, or changing the singer you listen to and more.

I hope that helps you re-think how *you* can take control of the influences in your life, and not just expect all influences to come from family, teachers and work colleagues or managers.

Story

When my son started to understand the power of change, he changed his diet, his hygiene, his clothing style, and his mindset. He also began seeing changes in his friendships.

He found that people who were hanging around for the wrong reasons started to get scared of his newfound integrity, and went else-where, giving him more peace to find himself even more. He began to focus on the real values of friendship and paying more attention to the people that mattered more at that time. Then one of his friends within a few weeks said...

"I've realised hanging around with Matt makes me a better person."

That was a powerful statement, said straight to me, in front of my son. What do you think that did to his self-

esteem?

Of course, it made him feel really great! He realised at last that making changes in himself would not leave him outcast and lonely, but finally appreciated by the right people, who ultimately made him feel even more valued the more he grew.

....

If you are always trying to be normal, you will never know how amazing you can be.
Maya Angelou

....

Stop worrying about trying to fit in, and just be yourself. I absolutely guarantee, the right people will love you and surround you when you can...

BE UNAPOLOGETICALLY YOU!

Before I move on, I want to follow this last quote with a piece about Self-Love.

You may think it sounds a strange concept to love yourself, but why would you expect other people to love what you don't? Why wouldn't you love what they love?

When you try to change for the benefit of friends, you alienate the people who truly love you for *you* – such as your family. Unless you have an unfortunate family background, your family will be in your life more than anyone else. When you lose friends, make friends, change schools or jobs, your family are still there. But even when you grow up and move out, at times when your family are not there in the room, why wouldn't you love yourself?

If you can be the person you truly want, and be passionate about a subject – any subject, that can find you a purpose in life; you will be happier with yourself as well.

If you are unhappy about living with anxiety, learn about it and create changes to instil calm such as meditation and yoga. You can still do other hobbies, but you will feel better about them if you can find your inner peace first.

Pamper yourself rather than expect someone else to do it. Go on walks and be mindful in nature. Watch videos online for inspiration, or read books, blogs or listen to podcasts, but when doing so, recognise that you are giving time to yourself, to sit and enjoy *your* time.

Use affirmations and positive self-talk – after all, why would you say something to yourself, that you would be upset if someone else said to you?

If there's one book I would recommend to follow this, it will be a book called "What to say when you talk to yourself." It has certainly helped me to rethink the things I tell myself, and boosted my confidence and self-belief into overcoming a traumatic year, quicker and with a forward focus on 'what *to do*' rather than constantly reflecting on 'what went wrong'.

Setting Social Goals

If only I could write an entire book on each change, there would be so much to say about social life alone, from beating the bullies, to falling in love, dealing with breakups, changing work, dealing with new managers, and reconnecting that spark with parents now you're no longer a child.

Think about firstly, what having a social life means to you. How many friends is enough? How many friends can you honestly spare time for without sacrificing your own quality of life?

Thinks about the type of settings you enjoy socialising in. Some people prefer a party atmosphere where others prefer a quieter or more structured social setting. Personally, I like meeting people through business events and networking, especially if they have great leadership or inspirational qualities, whatever their job.

Think about if you need a mentor or someone to support you

with your current learning or career journey. Who would you like to inspire YOU?

How would you like the relationship to change between you and your parents? As a couple, or individually, or maybe how you can improve the connection between you and a carer or step-parent if necessary.
Think back to the two lists of five people, and use these questions to identify where on your list of five, you would like to possibly put some focus on a different person to influence your life.

Also, think about communication and how people react to the way you speak to them. Is there anything you can do to speak more clearly, or swear less, or use a more confident tone of voice? What else could you improve in your communication skills?

EXERCISE 32:

WHAT IS YOUR NEW SOCIAL CHALLENGE?

Use your own intuition – after all, you are your own expert and growing better at it all the time – to set at least one goal to work on, for improving your social life, or your social skills.

_____

_____

_____

_____

Are you focusing on *you* as you set these goals? Remember they are about making changes in yourself – and then being aware of the way others change around you as a result.

Parent Toolbox

Social skills are the most difficult challenge around anxiety because so many teenagers fear that judgement and humiliation. There is also that element of feeling judged by you for the friends they do choose. Be aware of supporting their choices, and nurture them to find their own self-worth and their friendships will align naturally.

Another tip I would strongly recommend is to agree at the start of a conversation, that this is you mentoring, rather than mothering. It's a big transition for you too as your teenager grows up, but important to acknowledge this, so it doesn't drive you further apart.

Remember they are growing up, and they have probably been working towards this expectation of independence, due to being told to do things for themselves or to wait till they get to eighteen, and it brings a looming sense of life-shift.

They also feel the natural need to break free of mothering, even long before they are ready in today's society – because of the emotional cycle that our caveman brain still uses that would drive them through the emotions of fleeing the nest. In some countries, children are still sold off to marriage way too young as if still living in the cave days. That is another social challenge that many charities are trying to resolve.

By focusing on moving from mothering to mentoring, and making it clear that this is 'their' journey, but you are here when needed, it is much easier and more pleasant to sit and have open conversations about anything. Making time specifically to do this, is important because time gives value, along with your dedicated attention.

Key Points

Every action, reaction, or interaction you have with people has an effect on your emotions and theirs. How you utilize these is a choice. Knowing when you can make changes, and when you need help, is as important in social interactions and your resulting emotions, as it would be if a car were to break down.

Don't ever feel shame in having to request that you speak to someone like a teacher, counsellor, or even phone a charity if a social interaction has left you feeling broken.

If I can write this book and still need counselling to overcome the breakup of my marriage, then why would you deny yourself the chance of help? The chance to work through those emotions more quickly and positively, to find happiness again. Don't stay stuck, stay with it and grow from the changes.

Remember that roses grow in dirt, but the prize ones grow from added shit!

Now you have the knowledge of options and completed chapter two; you are armed with skills to change your life. Take time to sit and have conversations with someone responsible who enjoys sitting down to have an open conversation with you.

Remember that awareness is the first and most crucial step to making changes, and be aware of the things you say, think and share in your conversations. Also listen actively to the other person, whether it's a parent, teacher, manager or a friend, and listen to the words or phrases they use that are about changes and options.

If you hear them talk about positive changes, try and raise a compliment or a positive response. If they talk about negative things, try and just listen.

Just making this change in your conversation, to listen and be aware, will change how you feel about other people, about yourself, and soon – as my son did – you will see how people change for the better around you and towards you too.

"There are three things hard: Steel, A diamond, and to know one's self."

Benjamin Franklin 1706 – 1790
Founding Father of United States

CHAPTER 3: ROOT CAUSE

How would you like to drill down your options further, to find the root cause of change and find keys to making real and meaningful changes in your life?

We need to find the root causes of success rather than the root causes of failure.

In chapter one, we learned about the importance of *becoming aware* of a problem. After all, how can you fix a problem you are not aware exists? We did this by raising awareness of your four core emotions and how we change between emotions because something changed.

In chapter two, we looked at what changed, and the five options that H.E.L.P.S. you create your own powerful changes in your life.

In chapter three, we are going to look at how every Change, positive, negative, inner or outer, has one of only five root causes. Learning these will give you the keys to reversing change so that emotional awareness …

H.E.L.P.S. your life take F.L.I.T.E.

This is the third part of the Mood Mentor Model, and when you put all this together, you really can start to feel the difference in your mindset.

5 STEP MODEL FOR F.L.I.T.E.

Think of finding the root cause, as finding the START of a problem, then realise that the word START is also a great point for setting goals and targets, beginning new journeys, or if solving problems, the beginning of the end because when you find that starting point, the journey turns around for the better. This is the point where you DISCOVER—the point where you find your way, your purpose, your dreams, and your skills.

When you take these starting points, focus on your dreams, hone in on your skills, and then apply all the theories of change – guess what? YOU have the POWER to change your life in any direction you want.

When you know all that – why would you want to keep making the wrong changes?

OK, some people, situations and circumstances in life will still change for the worse. There's a massive difference between having the power to change, or trying to control and manipulate everything, but here's where you can learn to spot those root causes early on, and prevent as much negative change as possible and even avoid some changes. Others cannot be avoided at all, and you will soon understand what to do when you find a root cause, but the key to turning things around maybe a different key to the one that got you here.

Now when people tell you there's light at the end of the tunnel, you will know there are doors in that tunnel, creating barriers, and some are locked. The difference is, you now know how to change this and open the right doors. You will also learn which key to use for each door in life, to find your way to the light.

FINANCE

Have you ever heard the saying that money is the root of all evil? To a degree, money is the root of some evil, but money is also the root of happiness. Money buys gifts, pays bills, helps charities to help all kinds of causes, and money is the one thing most adults get stressed about not having enough of.

....

Anyone who thinks money will make you happier hasn't got money.
Davide Geffen

....

Looking At Finance As A Root Cause

It's easy enough to understand that money is the root of theft and fraud, also the root cause behind muggings and murders, blackmail and embezzlement, all creating crimes that are evil and unpleasant for anyone affected by the loss of money, items of value, or their health as a result of the crime and stress.

It is also easy to understand that not having enough money to pay the bills is another root cause of stress. Not having enough for that school ski-trip, is the root to poor children standing out, making them targets for bullying. The cost of school uniforms, or going to university, are all additional stress factors around money and growing up for you and your parents.

Also, being rich can have similar effects, putting social pressure on keeping up a certain image. It can be why some parents are so focused on money that children get sent to boarding school and suffer anxiety and loneliness from feeling unwanted, or like they are a lower priority than their parents work. Money is also the reason they have the opportunity to travel young and have access to a great education. The emotions last longer than the money and can be valued more when enjoyed.

Money and finance, however, are also the roots that grows incredible people and friendships. Giving a gift to someone gives greater value than the gift itself. Giving money to charity gives hope for a better future, and throwing a penny in a well buys a wish, which reinforces great beliefs that something miraculous is possible.

Finances is a better term to help understand that money is also currency, trade, value, transactions, accounts, and other terminology associated with the loss and gains, joys and pitfalls of dealing with one of the most complex global systems of economies, while also being as simple as gifting pocket money to a child.

Inner And Outer Changes To Your Finances

Inner changes around finance happen with your own skills around maths or your confidence in dealing with money. Are you emotionally attached to money and prefer putting it in the bank? Or do you prefer spending it and getting a good bargain for your money instead?

Money can be a fear for some people. They fear being without money and work relentlessly, stressing so much, they become ill and die before retirement, while others fear having money because they fear being hated for being successful.

Whatever way you look at money, or feel about your worth in your job role, or how you spend or save it, is all about your inner changes. There is no right or wrong answer, just finding the answers that make you happy and confident with the money you earn, spend and save, and the value of gifts you give and receive.

Money can be lost and found, earned, gambled, stolen, gifted, invested, traded for other currencies, and it can be both real and conceptual. These are outer changes, but it can also be an inner root cause for stress and happiness, hatred and joy.

Money can also be the key to many problems too, such as paying the dentist for a filling, or the vet for helping your pet get better. It pays for a haircut, books, well, you get the idea. It's endless, and it is important.

Story

My daughter was once asked if she had any hobbies, and she quickly replied, "Yes, I collect money."

The lady laughed, but then realised she wasn't joking. She went on to explain how she collected old coins, as well as runs of new coins in varying designs.

As my daughter was approaching her 18th birthday, her nan phoned to ask what she would like for her birthday. I immediately knew the answer because of a conversation that very morning over breakfast.

She had told me about a dream. She said "I was walking with a crowd of people and it was muddy, but then I looked down and saw an old Henry VIII coin in the mud. I picked it up, and then I WOKE UP! I actually had the coin in my hand and was excited, then woke up and didn't have it anymore." she finished with a sad face. So of course, I told her nan about the coin in her dream, and she was able to find an old Henry VIII coin on eBay.

How valuable do you think the gift of this coin was?

The value wasn't about the cost of the coin. It was about the thoughtfulness and the connection with her dream and her love of collecting coins. That was more valuable to her, along with the effort her nan had put in to find it, and the fact that we had listened to her dream.

Now is the time to start linking the Keys below, back to the Options in chapter two, by recognising how each one is both the root cause of a problem and can be the key to success.

Why Finance Is A Key To Life

Root Cause: What problems are you having when money or finances or adding stress to your life? Is it holding you back in your career? Taking too long to save for something really important? Or something that you struggle to keep in your pocket, heading straight for the shops at the first opportunity to fill your wardrobe with the latest branded goods? By recognising the correlation between finances and your emotional colour, you can begin to recognise the positive changes and goals that you could set for yourself to improve on these areas.

Keys: Which areas of life are you finding your finances most beneficial? Are you comfortably living with your parents and not yet having to worry about this? Are you confident in saving pocket money for a future nest egg? Are you interested in finances as a career option and confident in your ability with mathematics? Which areas of finances you have strengths, and how can you build these further to ensure a secure future?

EXERCISE 33:

Think about how your finances can help or hinder you with every option in the previous chapter and list one example of each:

	Root Cause	Key
H	_____	_____
E	_____	_____
L	_____	_____
P	_____	_____
S	_____	_____

....

You are the root of your financial success or failure. If you work on the roots, the fruits will take care of themselves.
T. Harv Eker

....

Setting Financial Goals

Think about setting yourself a financial goal. This could be anything from saving for some special trainers to learning a new career skill or buying a car. No matter how big or small make it relevant to your circumstances and skills around finances. You can set more goals throughout your whole life.

What financial goals would you like to set?

_____

_____

_____

What is your current status?

_____

_____

_____

What steps do you need to take in between?

_____

_____

_____

If necessary, write the steps out in a series of smaller steps, and break them down into as many smaller manageable steps as possible, on a separate piece of paper.

Parent Toolbox

Finances can be a very difficult subject for teenagers to grasp when going through depression, or very confusing and frustrating trying to set up all necessary bills and read all the legal regulations when moving into their own adult life.

If you are comfortable helping them through this, try to keep conversations on a calm mindset. If you struggle to have financial conversations with your teenager and find one of you becoming irritable, it may be worth asking someone else if they would be willing to support them through these challenging times. A financial mentor of sorts.

Key Points

Finances can be a very big emotional barrier, especially for someone who is not very good with numbers. If you are good with computers, there are ways to manage finances without the stress adding up, keeping account of the monthly bills.

Personally, I set all my monthly bills out in a spreadsheet and use the autosum function to do all the calculations. All I have to do then is ensure the direct debits are set up, and the bills are paid. And money in the account of course.

If you are looking to invest money, save from early towards a mortgage, or get involved in any business set up, always seek plenty of advice from reputable business groups and people who have been there before rather than going in blindly. Making a bad investment or business decision is equally emotional destructive as the excitement received from making good ones. If in doubt, keep your money out.

LINKS

Links are the connections between two or more separate things. This can be the link between friends, the link between knowledge and missing information, or the link between two pieces of wiring.

Family are linked through genetics, as a family tree, and in their social bonds. Family can also suffer hurt and pain when these links are broken, such as adoption, or separation, losing a life, or through a family fall out. Whether whole or broken, it is the connections that make your family.

A connection is anything where items, people, information, or scenarios meet, either intentionally, or through impact. Sometimes a positive impact when information is shared correctly, can connect people to what they need. My hope is that this book has a positive impact on you, now that you are connected with it. Connections also need fixing, and this is where skills and tradeable commodities fall under these five categories. Accountants help fix people's finances. They become a powerful business connection that helps link income and outgoings together with the law.

Doctors help link symptoms with root causes of health and then link their medical information to the solution to help you get well again.

A clock, a calendar, and alarm, a stop-watch and timetables, are all examples of ways to link time with other things happening in life like the time you need to be at a class or appointment, or the time your favourite TV show is on next. These tools help you link dates with birthdays and holidays. Imagine being anywhere on time if there were no tools to link time with your plans and goals.

Logic is applying what you already know to new and existing puzzles and situations. It is also the link between what you know and what you don't know when a connection is missing.

As strange as that may sound, when you are faced with a problem, and don't know the answer, the only thing you can do is reflect on what you do already know such as 'who' might already know the answer or 'where' you can get spare parts or 'why' this worked before or 'what' you saw happen in a similar situation in that movie last week.

....

Goals are the links in the chain that connect activity to accomplishment

Zig Ziglar

....

Looking At Links As A Root Cause

Looking for Connections as a root cause can be as simple as looking for a broken part or as complex as finding a broken link in a corporate process such as an information leak, a failure to follow a part of the process, money being wasted unnecessarily, people not communicating effectively, why people are taking time off sick, or something else that is missing entirely. They may be failing to advertise correctly to connect with the right customers or failing to share the correct information about their products and services.

For you, this process of finding a root cause may be about why a friend stopped talking to you – and what information they heard. It may be your health, or you may want to work on improving it. Maybe you want to go to university and need information and contacts for getting in touch with the campus, and then connecting with an estate agent to find suitable accommodation.

Connecting what you learn with your future career is called practice, and during this, there will be lots of failures and broken links, but remember that every failure is a learning curve. Every learning curve is growth, and growth is the best success of all.

Inner And Outer Changes To Your Links

Inner Changes: An easy way to think of inner connections is remembering and forgetting information. This can also be knowing, or thinking you know, then realising you were wrong, or you learn something new.

Your inner connections to people change as they say things to build or break your trust. Your thoughts and beliefs and values are all constantly changing as you learn, for example, you may value a limited-edition album from your favourite singer, then learn the singer committed a crime. Does your internal value of the record change? Most likely, it will.

Every time you look at the album or listen to their songs, it reminds you of something terrible. You no longer hold it in personal value. This is a separate value than the one we talked about in finance because it is more about the connection you hold with it emotionally.

This is the connections you make through your thoughts, feelings, and beliefs you hold about everything, and everyone, including yourself. It's how you personally value the world. Understanding your emotional connections through these thoughts, feelings, and beliefs, can help you re-evaluate them to discover which sets of values are helping you, and which ones are holding you back.

Outer Changes: Being bumped into, your pushbike chain falling off, your shoelaces coming undone, finding directions on a map to where you want to be, or washing your clothes when they are dirty, are all about connections too.

Being bumped into is a temporary and accidental physical connection. Your bike chain falling off has become disconnected and needs to be reconnected. Shoelaces lose tension, and the connection falls apart, just as dirt stuck on your clothes can be washed out again – mostly.

Glue and tape join the ranks of nuts and bolts among a whole engineering world of physical connections while solder and switches make up just a part of the electronic world of connections.

These examples are just enough to get you thinking about just how many connections there are in this world, from every scientific and conceptual angle imaginable.

Story

Probably the best story I can share here is why I wrote this book. At 18 years old, my son struggled with the comprehension of any concepts like time and money. He was deeply depressed and barely connected with life. He certainly wasn't connected to his own emotional awareness, even denying that the emotional state he was in could be improved.

I was acting like an emotional paramedic, on call 24/7 for his emotional breakdowns, and often taking three hours to talk him out of the deepest darkest depressions. As much as I could talk him out of them, I somehow couldn't prevent him from going back in. How was I supposed to help him?

We had tried self-help books, talking, videos, therapy and more, but nothing seemed to help. That's when I realised, I needed a 'visual' way to teach him about emotions, but there was nothing available.

They say, 'Necessity is the Mother of Invention,' and that's when this mother had a real necessity to keep her son alive and start teaching him to manage his own emotions - because I couldn't do it for him for the rest of his life.

That is when I started using colours to connect his awareness to his actual emotions. It's when I started to connect my own understanding of emotional patterns to life in general and realised, I could use it to connect with you by creating this book.

Now it is your turn to connect all this information to your life, and when it starts working, pay it forward by telling others how it helps you. Remember some of it will be changes you can make quickly, while some will be lifelong learning, but the system is still the system, just as time is time and they will both serve you a lifetime.

Why Links Is A Key To Life

Links are what holds everything together. From atoms to the global economy. If you don't know what holds anything together, from friendships and families, or bikes to buildings, how can you recognise what is broken? Or what needs fixing? What needs nurturing and maintaining regularly? Or what links and connections hold the most value?

Sometimes there are links or connections you need to remove. A rusty link on a loose bike chain, or a toxic friendship. A job that's creating burnout, or a bill that's draining your bank for that gaming membership you no longer use.

Making that connection between things that are making life better and things that are draining your life and emotions, is an important step that helps you really dig deep, to discover the real root cause of your emotions and what the potential solutions are. Dig deep enough, and you *will* dig up those keys to FLITE.

EXERCISE 34:

Think about how your Links or Connections can help or hinder you with every option in the previous chapter and list one example of each:

	Root Cause	Key
H	_____	_____
E	_____	_____
L	_____	_____
P	_____	_____
S	_____	_____

....

The real value of setting goals is not the recognition or reward, it's the person we become by finding the discipline, courage and commitment to achieve them.
Unknown

....

Setting Linked Goals

Think about setting yourself goals about Links. No matter how big or small make it relevant to your circumstances and skills around connections.

What is the goal you want to set?

_____

_____

_____

What is your current status?

_____

_____

_____

What steps do you need to take in between?

_____

_____

_____

If necessary, write the steps out in a series of smaller steps, and break them down into as many smaller manageable steps as possible, on a separate piece of paper.

Parent Toolbox

It's an impossible task to expect a teenager or even an adult to learn everything in the world about connections, but it helps to have as many conversations as possible about the Ins and outs of their life and your family life, to identify as many connections as possible space in an outer, physical and non-tangible.

The key here is not learning every solution in the world but learning to recognise the patterns that raised logic around connections in general.

Playing board games, watching, and discussing films, helping with homework or inspiration for their new job role, can all help connect their mind and awareness with how connected or disconnected everything else is in life.

Key Points

Concepts is a great way to think about the keys to F.L.I.T.E. that link emotional connections with non-physical solutions. For example, the connection in energy between two people is not tangible, yet it is thought of as being real through love and hate.

The concept of time is connected to reality by making it visible on a clock while the measurement is scaled out on a ruler, tape measure, or through mathematical equations that calculate the distance of stars – connecting the knowledge of the universe. Also remember that connections link ALL the categories in this book and can be temporary or permanent, physical, or conceptual, positive or negative, purposeful or accidental, valued or detrimental, barriers or keys to success.

INFORMATION

How do you know what you don't know?

At first thought, information may appear to be nothing but positive. Information is knowledge and knowledge is power, so therefore it is possible to think that knowledge is all good?

What about gossip? Surely false information or shared information with malicious intent is not good information.

The information has many useful purposes. For example, purchasing the latest games console requires instructions on how to set up, activate, and play. How useful would the games console be if you didn't know no how to get it up and running? The instructions are important to the value of the product.

Purchasing a new hair dye requires instructions on the box for how to prepare your hair, apply the dye, the time to let it react with your hair and clear instructions for rinsing it out again. How helpful is it when the box doesn't mention possible reactions with previous hair products, and your hair turns an unexpected shade of orange or green?

Missing information or incorrect information is frequently the root cause of some very frustrating problems in life, like the time your teacher is asking for homework, but you missed the information on what homework to do. Imagine if you went shopping and nothing had prices on it, not even the receipt. How would you know what you are spending?

Science, on the other hand, is all about finding missing information. Searching the skies for unknown stars and planets. Scavenging the earth for new and unknown elements. Mixing countless chemicals and biological elements in the lab for new and unknown substances or medicines with all kinds of uses stronger glues for space crafts, to cancer cures, and more recently Covid-19 vaccines.

News Is also information about current and relevant topics and maybe urgent or important to share, as well as touching on inspirational news.

Stories and films can be fact or fictional information that can connect you with the past, as well as the present and the future. They can tell you of history, culture, beliefs and dreams. They can also use fables and fairy tales to help you learn lessons about behaviour in yourself and others as examples, but the genres of films and books are very varied. Why not look at some titles and see how they connect with the theories in this book?

Information can be shared freely, withheld on purpose – particularly when someone covers a crime, or it can be charged for such as from lawyers, or as a book. Libraries on the other hand are there to help everyone connect with knowledge because of its sheer importance, and loan books out for free.

Police and investigators seek information, while the law sets out information in ways that should be followed to keep the peace. A judge has to make a decision on the information provided while teachers try and help you learn as much information as possible.

The problem with information, though is it can make your brain feel like a compression chamber when everything is going in, and nothing is coming out. This is why sports, games, conversation, friends and voluntary work, are all good at helping you release some of that tension, so you can continue learning.

There's also personal information or confidential information as well as the type of information that computers use to know your habits and advertise everything possible at every encounter online. Learning to ignore a lot of this information and not be distracted by it can be as frustrating as what you are actually looking for. Also, social media platforms have learned that they can charge you to take it away, as well as charging the person putting it up there. How annoying!

....

Knowledge comes from learning but Wisdom comes from living.

Anthony Douglas Williams

....

All knowledge is greater understood when put to practice. This reminds me of a Chinese proverb that I absolutely love, and it says...

"What I hear I forget.
What I see I remember.
What I do, I understand."

Looking At Information As A Root Cause

When faced with a challenge or a choice, and you think you have looked at all the options, but feeling stuck, there is a quote that my good friend and humorous speech contest winner James McGinty shared with me as his favourite. It is...

....

When everything you are sure of doesn't work, then something you're sure of must be wrong.

....

It makes perfect sense that if nothing works, it's not that nothing will ever work, it's because you are missing some information. The question is, where? That's what the H.E.L.P.S., F.L.I.T.E. categories will help you with. Eliminate everything you do know, and find what category you don't know. It helps narrow down the missing options.

Imagine your dad's car broke down. What information are you missing?

Let's look at the options for finding out why information is key.

You can get the manual out of the glove box – that has 'some' information in it, but if that fails, you can call the breakdown. You need their phone number to call, and that's information too. Then you have to give them information – the registration number, where you are broken down etc.

If you don't have breakdown cover, is there a friend you can call? Or a local garage? Or if you're in a hurry to get going and don't have breakdown cover at home, is it possible to fix something small yourself by finding information on the internet?

Several things to consider are, how much information you already know, how much you want to know, and who else knows?

Also if you had the knowledge, would you be able to do anything with it? After all, the knowledge may be useless without the spare parts and tools. That takes you back to who you know with tools, or where you can get the spare parts – more information needed.

It's all information, and it's about connecting it all together to find a solution. So next time you think school or work is hard, just realise how much information you rely on all the time. It's more collectable than superhero comics, and just as valuable when you have the right information.

Inner And Outer Changes To Your Information

Information changes you when you learn it. Sometimes it enlightens you, helps you find fun and enjoyment or helps you become smarter. Information can make you happier and make life easier. Your favourite recipe, for example, or the knowledge that a new film is due out at the cinema is good information, as much as the skills you learn about.

A great example is woodwork. It's physical, but it's also learning about the types of wood, how to best use the tools and understanding the meanings on the diagrams for new projects that all hold information to help you learn and grow internally to achieve your skill.

Other times you can forget things, or not understand them, get confused, and feel frustrated. You may get lost and need a map or navigation system. Hearing bad news or having to follow regulations – especially all those terms and conditions that come with everything these days. Information can become a major overload or be required by tight deadlines.

Listening is a really important skill in the art of taking in information. Listening is a skill that continues to grow, while sometimes misinformation can be heard. It's funny when you hear a song but mishear the lyrics, but it's also powerful when you hear more than the words and hear the real message behind them.

It's also frustrating when you misheard instructions from your parents, teachers or boss; then we are shouted at because you either hadn't listened properly or had failed to ask them to repeat the information to be sure you were doing the right thing. We will come back to this more in the category of Social Skills.

These examples may be about external information you receive but the point to understand is HOW it changes your internal perception of that information, how it affects your emotions, your actions, your thoughts, your beliefs, and the consequences of missing or incorrect information, as well as the power of getting the right information.

External information sources are the million road signs to read on a journey, that billboard that changes every time you pass it, or the timetable at the bus stop being updated learning new topics at school or training for a new role at work.

As well as written and visual information, there is also audible information, new stories your parents share of past memories or a message on your answerphone. Being corrected on something you had misunderstood, or being praised, complimented and appreciated for something you said right, or for the clothes you are wearing today? How did the information received, affect your emotions?

This is all external information and remember that mastering life is all about mastering change? What happens when you are blind? You switch visual for audible or tactile. Sensory information is another source – using shapes and textures to tell us about objects. Temperature, size, colour and other factors, all make up information about objects and substances around you.

Stop reading for just two minutes, and see how much information you can find, only by looking ahead of you over the top of this book. If it's a wall, see how much information you can make out about the structure, texture, colour, and the stories that wall has held over the years.

Story

I mentioned earlier about a Steamship Captain who used his logic to project manage a cable laying mission. His name was Captain Benjamin Gleadell, and he had to have impeccable listening skills in his role, listening throughout his career to the crew, passengers, and the sounds of the ships he sailed. He required lots of information about the workings of the ship, the stars for navigation, and particularly the weather at sea, as well as how the ship was being run or how the passengers were being kept safe.

On one occasion, Benjamin's listening skills surpassed even the expectations of everyone who knew him. It was incredibly foggy at sea, and they were ten miles out of Boston Harbour in Ireland when he thought he heard a dog barking. His crew simply thought he was barking mad.

Benjamin was convinced he heard this dog, even though no one else could hear it. He had two options. He could listen to his own intuition and the knowledge that a dog shouldn't be in the sea, or he could listen to the other people around him who thought it was impossible for a dog to be in the sea.

Benjamin chose to listen to his intuition and knew from the tone that the dog was barking for help. He ordered the ship to be steered off course in search of the noise.

Sure enough, after a short while and ten miles out to sea, they found the dog.

There was a man in a rowing boat who had got lost in the fog and been drifting further and further out to sea for several hours. Benjamin and his crew rescued the man and the dog, which was an Old English Sheep Dog.

The man in the rowing boat was fully aware that had Benjamin not listened to the dog barking, or had the weather turned the seas rough, or he drifted further to sea, he may never have been found. All knowledge that had him fearing for his life.

Just as we talked earlier about value, the man valued so much, the listening skills of Benjamin, and the effort to sail off course and rescue him and his dog, that he wanted to give Benjamin a gift. The only thing he had with him was his dog.

Benjamin took the Old English Sheep Dog home to his family of five children, and the dog became one of their family for the rest of his happy, tail-wagging life.

So you see how information is about more than just written words, it's about piecing together everything you do and don't know – to find a happy ending.

Why not read this story with a parent or friend, and discuss how much other information the story tells you? See how far you can take the conversation beyond the words written above.

Why Information Is A Key To Life

Information is not only a key to creating an incredible life and solving countless problems, but it's also a key to being human. Look at how information has been passed through thousands of years of history, through stone tablets, scrolls, books, songs, and stories.

The nature of passing on information has changed with the creativity of every artist, the progression of languages and styles of music, the invention of photography, filmography, electronics, and the internet.

There is no excuse for saying *'There's no way!"* or
"It's I'm possible."

If it has been done before, you need to connect with the right information. If it has not been done before, there's new information to be found and connected. Something is only truly impossible if it has been scientifically proven to be impossible. Otherwise, it is simply knowledge that is not part of your learning, yet.

EXERCISE 35:

Think about how Information can help or hinder you with your challenges for each option in the previous chapter, and list one example of each:

	Root Cause	Key
H	_____	_____
E	_____	_____
L	_____	_____
P	_____	_____
S	_____	_____

···

All information is good, even when it is bad.
Proverb

···

Although this may not be literally true for you, there is the element of staying safe and avoiding danger, where bad information helps you avoid the pitfalls of life. Be aware of what bad information is helpful, and how it helps to know it.

Setting Information Goals

Think about setting yourself an information goal, no matter how big or small make it relevant to your circumstances and skills around learning new information.

What is the goal you want to set?

_____

_____

_____

What is your current status?

_____

_____

_____

What steps do you need to take in between?

_____

_____

_____

If necessary, write the steps out in a series of smaller steps, and break them down into as many smaller manageable steps as possible, on a separate piece of paper.

Parent Toolbox

Helping your teenager or young adult to learn about information can be a great way of taking conversations to the next level, and helping them value your experiences, also in recognising that even when you don't know the answers, you may have the contacts for people who do.

Ensuring that your teenager has access to good quality information either at the library, online, or even via documentary channels, will help them grow from all this information. If they want to learn about something more specialised, they may require outside support, access to groups, or a mentor to help them.

Ensuring they have connections to information that inspires them, will massively grow their confidence and sense of self-worth. Also remember that expecting them to learn a subject that is not their main passion, even with the good intentions of a stable career, can do as much harm as good to their self-worth, confidence, and ability to find happiness in life. What worked for you may not work for them.

Lastly, using the story in this chapter, seeing how much non-spoken information can be filled in by further conversation is a powerful way to connect the art of conversation with fun and inspiration.

Key Points

As we are on the topic of information, it is important to realise that the information in this book is just the tip of the iceberg when it comes to learning about life. There are countless self-help books and online mentors that can help you more specifically with confidence, anxiety, personality disorders, relationships, careers, selling, how to learn and retain more information and more.

This book will help you see a pattern in emotions; just the way school teaches you times-tables. If you learn enough to help you understand your own emotions, it's a win. If you learn more and help others, it's a success at any level.

While some people learn enough maths to work in a shop, maths patterns are infinitely complex way beyond even my comprehension, leading to complex scientific equations. Emotions can be thought of the same way.

There are counsellors, psychologist, sociologists, cognitive behavioural therapists, neurosurgeons, meditation gurus and so many more, that all interpret and understand information about emotions in different ways and at highly different levels of knowledge.

How much has this book sparked your interest in your knowledge of emotions?

TIME

How much value do you put on time? Time to sleep, time to eat, time to learn, time with family and time to simply have fun?

Time is an enigma that has fascinated humans for thousands upon thousands of years. Every person has a finite amount of time on earth and has no knowledge of the exact date and time their life will end. Other than this, every living human has the exact same 24 hours in every day of their life. What we do with that time is what matters.

Time is said to be a great healer - both physically and emotionally. As this book is all about emotional healing, let's look at the importance of time on your emotions.

Memories about times you remember both good and bad, affect

how you think and feel even today. In a perfect world, you would like every day to become good memories for the future. Thankfully you have this book underway to learn this skill, but you also need to realise there will be times that cannot be avoided.

Getting up on time, being at school or work on time, times when we lose loved ones, times you are sick, and times when people hurt your feelings, are all about snippets of time, but your life encompasses a broader expanse of time.

I once heard a lady explain that there are two dates on a tombstone. The date you were born and the date you died but the most important part of those dates was the dash in the middle. That's the time of your life that really matters, the part between the dates.

What are you doing with your dash?

Time creates sensations of passing quickly when you're having fun or passing slowly when you are bored sad or can't wait to get out of a difficult situation, yet time is a fixed constant of seconds minutes hours weeks months and years. The years are grouped into decades centuries and millennia. It's strange that no matter how much time passes, it can still be condensed into a single word.

Looking at how time helps you with life's challenges gives you the power to manage that time more effectively and create more positive times in your life. It gives you the power to give time to others, spend time taking care of you first, invest time in your education, take time to heal emotionally and physically, and who measured time out effectively when setting goals, by using time to create mini-goals in between.

It is said to take 90 days for a new habit to set in but 90 days seems like a massive challenge when starting out on a life-changing new habit whether that's exercising, changing your diet, or cutting back on something like cigarettes.

By breaking down this target into three months and setting smaller goals for each month with a lesser reward at each step, makes the larger goal seem more accessible.

You can break each month down further into weekly goals and treat each day as a separate goal as well. If you miss a day, it may seem easy to just carry on, and except the last days of the target; however, I was given this advice just yesterday.

When you set the target, number every day of that target from 1 – 90, and if you feel like missing a day, ask yourself "How much do I love myself?"

If you miss a day, you have to **start again** at day one because it has to be 90 days consecutive, for the new habit to form and become a normal routine.

Just like some things take time to accomplish, some things take time away, like time to fix that broken car, or time to save up, or time to keep searching for a job. It takes set amounts of time to go through school and college, while other times are flexible.

Timing can be crucial, like the time it takes to rescue someone who has stopped breathing, while the time taken to relax on holiday is a luxury.

Looking At Time As A Root Cause

When you procrastinate over a job and leave everything to the last minute, or something happens that is urgent; time causes stress. Time and action (red emotions) always lead towards stress or excitement, but stress can be both positive and negative.

Some people thrive on pushing through deadlines and enjoying that massive rush of dopamine that comes with success, while others become sick when the stress is constant, never-ending, no goals or successes, but the daily drudge of simply keeping up.

If you're struggling with homework, exams, or a job, and finding it stressful, try assessing how you think about your time doing it. Can you break it down into smaller pieces?

Time can be that all-important barrier when missing the bus or finishing an exam paper. It can also be the key to taking time to plan. Leaving the house on time, or spending enough time studying before the exam, and not leaving everything to the last minute.

Say for example – I need to do three hours of homework, but for every hour, I will spend 5-10 minutes dancing to my favourite songs – going crazy!

This way, you set a smaller goal and get that dopamine rush from the enjoyment of music and movement. You may need to use your imagination if at work but finding any way of self-rewarding smaller time-snippets of work, helps to relieve the negative stress and build resilience.

Sorry to say it but taking a time-out for a cigarette break does not count, as it is counterproductive with negative health benefits.

When time no longer seems to matter, or you seem disconnected and lost in time, this may be the very time to evaluate just how overloaded your emotions may be and determine if you may be suffering depression.

Inner And Outer Changes To Your Time

When something is due to happen, and you associate it with uncertainty, no matter how far the time is in the future, this causes anxiety. This is an internal change around time and expectation. In fact, all emotions can be associated with time, both forward and backwards.

If you suffer anxiety, take time to breathe. Breathe deeply and with purpose. Exhale slowly, and allow your nerves to calm, reminding yourself that right now, at this moment in time, you are safe. These inner changes are caused by having time to think about things.

On the flip side of anxiety is excitement, like the times you can't wait for your next birthday, Christmas, or other family celebration, depending on your religion and culture.

If you're into sports, maybe it's the next world cup, or the next gymnastics competition you are taking part in. It is the time leading up to the event that builds excitement and expectations of happy memories.

Parents use this concept between anxiety and excitement, to help children overcome the fear of going to the dentist by promising them a treat if they are good during the check-up.

You can use this same strategy to set your own goals as a teenager or adult too. Why not? If it helps in any way to overcome that anxiety and have a positive goal to look forward to, beyond the challenge in question, then love yourself and embrace the challenge. Just remember to be careful about your financial goals in the process.

Outer changes to time might be a friend being late to pick you up for the cinema, or having taken time off for an appointment, only for the appointment to be cancelled last minute. Sometimes you cannot find enough time to complete tasks, or maybe someone helps you to complete it sooner.

Being aware of time helps you recognise when time is a barrier, so you can adapt your schedule or workload, or ask for help. Other times you have too much time on your hands and get bored easily. Finding things to fill time becomes the new challenge instead.

Time to rest your mind is the most important time of all. Treat it like a muscle that needs to be exercised, and the more you train it, the stronger it becomes, but like a real muscle, it also needs time to rest and recover. Brain strain is real too.

Story

When my son was finally grown up, coming out of the other side of depression and looking forward to the birth of his daughter, he took time to reflect on his life, and how his emotions had both held him back, deceived him through depression, and helped him to recover once he understood them.

He reflected on the times he had been depressed, and the times we had spent as a happy family. He reflected on the importance all this gave him with the date of his daughter's arrival getting close and said...

"I've been thinking about my role as a father and what I can teach my daughter. I've realised that the most important thing I can teach her is to manage her emotions. If I get that right, then everything else will fall into place for her."

How right could he be? I went from having a severely depressed son, to having an incredible young man with a whole new outlook on life. I also have a granddaughter who is the most boundless, energetic, happy, and resilient little girl, who sees nothing as impossible.

As a result of his time to reflect; at the back of this book is a picture of my granddaughter trying to reach her dad's pull-up bars.

She couldn't reach so got herself a little step and tried again. I'm sure she will continue trying till the day she can do it on her own. Instead of telling her to get down, he takes time to lift her up and lets her do her exercises before letting her down to run off with joy and laughter.

That is time well spent that will pay back in later years as her happy memories.

Why Time Is A Key To Life

If you don't think carefully about time, you will never use it wisely.

Time is a commodity, just like money. You can earn time and spend time. You can give time to someone, or they can give time to you. You can waste time or make the most of the time. You can pay for time such as at a concert, or at the dentist, or you can earn from your time by doing chores or getting a job.

Time can be stressful or joyful, hold value or be stolen from you.

Whatever you do with your time, be alert to how you are using it. Don't burn it out by using it ALL the time, and don't hoard time by never spending it on anything.

As much as time can be that horrendous barrier that has you running around brushing your teeth then leaving home in your slippers, time can also be your best friend. Take time to look after yourself as well as others and balance it well across all areas of life.

EXERCISE 36:

Think about how Time can help or hinder you with every option in the previous chapter and list one example of each:

	Root Cause	Key
H	_____	_____
E	_____	_____
L	_____	_____
P	_____	_____
S	_____	_____

....

The bad news is time flies. The good news is, you're the pilot.
Michael Altshuler

....

Setting Time Goals

Think about setting yourself a new Time goal, no matter how big or small make it relevant to your circumstances and skills around Timekeeping, or a goal that requires time input.

What is the goal you want to set?

_____

_____

_____

What is your current status?

_____

_____

_____

What steps do you need to take in between?

_____

_____

_____

If necessary, write the steps out in a series of smaller steps, and break them down into as many smaller manageable steps as possible, on a separate piece of paper.

Parent Toolbox

Just as this category talks about giving and receiving time, the time you spend with your teenager is most valuable when given one-to-one, with full attention. This is not saying you are not doing this, but many parents these days are busy running to and from work, receiving phone calls all evening, trying to catch up on housework and cook meals, and somewhere in between, holding half conversations with teenagers through bedroom doors, or passing like ships in the night. It's understandable that not everyone has the same time to dedicate but setting expectations – just like goals – for both your benefits, will help you move forward together. Even an agreed time for 5-10 minutes a day will make a massive difference for you both. When you give time to them, they give back.

When my son was in the deepest depression, he was already living in a hostel because I didn't have the right book for him, I didn't have this system, but I finally had the emotional time to myself, to help him too. I told him that I would phone him every single day until he sorted his life out. And I did phone him 'every' day. Some days we spoke for two minutes, some for much longer. It depended on his emotional state, but the lower he was, the more we talked till I knew he was safe.

I would invest that time any day, over worrying about a time he might have ended up in prison or a coffin instead.

When you say you don't have time, I simply beg you to be aware of why you are saying that. If you really don't have time for a valid reason, rather than not giving them time, who can? Who can you get to be there and check in on them every day, on the day's when you cannot?

Time can also be rearranged and prioritised – please don't let it be for a funeral.

Key Points

Just as in my parent toolbox tip, if you are feeling suicidal and that your time on earth is overwhelming, it's your responsibility to ASK for time. Ask your parents to take the time to listen. Ask a teacher, friend or better still, find the Samaritans phone number 116 123 and take time to call them.

Sometimes that little bit of time taken to talk, makes the world seem just bright enough to take one more step.

When my son came through depression, he said that those phone calls were like someone shining a torch in the dark for a couple of minutes a day. He said some days he knew he made progress, while on other days he didn't, but that light allowed him to see ahead just enough to plan for the following day again.

Be aware of how time is affecting your emotions, as well. If other people are not giving you the time you need – who else can give you that time? Can you talk with grandparents, aunts or uncles? Can you talk with a neighbourly friend?

Time will become your best friend when you learn to value it that way. Even when no one else has time for you, you have time for yourself. Be the friend you would want them to be and do something amazing with that time.

Take time to learn something new or take time out in nature, breathing fresh air.

Remember, it's what you do with the dash that counts.

Treat your emotions to time - like a cake in the oven.
Too little time and they will be mushy,
Too much and they will burn out.
Get it just right - and everyone will want a slice.
Kay Reeve

ENERGY

When you think of energy, do you automatically think of electricity? Or the energy used for running? What about all the other types of energy too?

Wow, my mental energy was flagging after writing 33,000 words in 9 days and was so busy I forgot to check my electricity meter. I then had to use my personal energy to walk to the shops and top up the credit token.

Home and powered up again, I put the kettle on, which transferred the energy to a lovely hot drink before getting back to the mental energy of writing again. But while all this energy is happening, my emotional energy is buzzing with the thoughts of my book being out in three weeks from now.

I've had a book coach and an agent who are mentoring me through and keeping my motivational energy topped up like a gas tank while my efforts are draining it at full speed again.

I've previously worked for an offshore energy company, and well aware of the power that comes from the wind, or the negative energy a community can create from fear and the positive energy that comes from great information and communication.

Before that, I used to sell fuel treatment and understand the purpose of combusting fuel to create compression to drive a vehicle. I understand the energy between people and how emotions create positive and negative energies that make-or-break relationships and friendships. Or how that energy is manipulated by the media and advertising.

What about how the universe is a constant flow of energy that helps the world turn every day and creates the appearance that the sun comes up and sets, while the moon comes out at nights and the stars shift with the seasons?

Have you learned about nuclear energy from the sun and the sheer intensity of sunburn from being out in the sun too long? I understand how we can flag and lose energy in the winter from too little exposure to the sun, and I thrive from being in the sun in spring and autumn on a long walk. Have you noticed how your energy changes when the sun comes out, even if you sit by a sunny window?

Have you thought about the energy that comes from the vibration of sound? How does music impact your emotional energy? Do you cry and the sad lyrics? Or do you prefer something to dance along to?

I love listening to vibrational music that is set to specific Hz frequencies for different energy levels within the body.

Food gives us energy, and junk food can steal your energy after a temporary hit of satisfaction. Your health is all about energy levels, and playing sports uses energy. At the same time, just enough can revitalise your energy levels by drawing in fresh oxygen and getting it pumping round in your blood.

There is so much energy in the world – there's more than enough for everyone. What types of energy are you tapping into to get your daily dose of dopamine?

....

Everything you do in life, either gives you energy or drains you of energy. Choose wisely.

Unknown

....

You are like a battery and every action, thought, or choice in life affects the energy levels in your emotional and physical battery levels. Choose positive thoughts to top up your battery and stop those negative thoughts draining it.

Looking At Energy As A Root Cause

Just as energy is great at powering items, bodies and minds, so it can stop them working too.

As mentioned below the previous quote, negative energy in the mind reduces the functionality of your brain and lowers your performance in many areas of life. Switching to positive thinking, and practising gratitude, mindfulness and meditation, or letting out that negative energy through sports, can help uplift your mind and bring back functionality to your life.

The energy in physical forms such as gas, electric or fuel in your car, can be connected, or disconnected, full or empty, contained or leaking. Depending on the problem, look for the root cause to ensure the energy flows again. Sometimes it is a simple as turning on the switch and laughing about the stress over nothing, while other times it may be more serious and require an electrician or other technician.

When it's your health that is lacking in energy, look at your diet, your exercise, your attention to breathing deeply and purposefully, and see a doctor if your energy is not returning, or dropped suddenly through illness.

Social energy is about the positive thoughts and how you share them, give them, receive them, and when not socially distanced, share hugs, shake hands, sit and talk with friends, or have a really good laugh together.

If your social energy is lacking, and you don't want to mix with other people, this may be a single day to rest, in which case I applaud you for taking care of yourself first. If the avoidance of others is too frequent, it is likely a sign of depression and may be time to talk to someone like a parent or teacher again, to get to the root cause of why.

Inner And Outer Changes To Your Energy

As much as there are lots to talk about with regards to energy and challenges in life, I want you to recognise that energy makes things work, and a lack of energy stops things working. Sometimes an energy overload can burn things out, or make them explode. Sometimes things are missing or broken, and everything can be fixed with the right knowledge. But today I want to focus on YOUR energy.

Think about the physical forms of energy and how you use these analogies to talk about your own energy.

Have you ever exploded, or felt burnt out?

Been left lifeless, or buzzing with energy?

Your personal emotional-energy is the very reason you are reading this book. This is the manual that will help you identify why your energy level is out of sync.

You can answer this now you understand the emotional cycle diagram of awareness on the back cover of this book. It is your own personal energy map. The orange is the wiring that allows energy to flow between the red, blue, black and ideally shine brightest in the yellow area. Ask yourself this...

Do I feel happy, sad, angry or depressed?

You might feel excited, or that you are falling in love, or contented sitting and talking to a friend, and they are all levels happiness. Different levels of emotional energy in the yellow section of the diagram.

You might feel anxious and nervous about exams, but that's worrying about feeling sad if you fail. You might feel fear or grief. These are all levels of energy in the blue section of the diagram.

You might feel angry and aggressive outwardly, or even just in thoughts, or you might feel lesser equivalents like frustrated, irritable, or snappy. These are all different energy levels in the red section of the diagram.

When you feel lost, hopeless, lifeless, depressed, lethargic, and completely lacking in the energy to do anything, this is depression. Yet, it can live along with stress and anxiety, grief and fear, aggression, and even being aware of some things that should make you happy. Like having the lights out, you know things are there but have no Energy to enjoy them.

Now try and work out what changed, and what you can do to bring that energy back.

Why Energy Is A Key To Life

When the electricity goes out at home, do you light candles? Or do you use a torch? Do you sit in the dark and wait?

What if you sat in the dark all night, waiting for the electric to come on again and then realised that although the lights aren't working, the fridge light comes on when you go to get milk for your breakfast in the morning?

Looking at WHY the energy has stopped, or not working properly is the only way it will get fixed.

If a light blew and tripped the circuit, you probably didn't need to sit in the dark all night. You can change the bulb and flip the trip-switch on again. On the other hand, if the whole house was without electric, instead of just changing a bulb yourself, you would have to wait for the electricity board to fix an overhead cable or something similar.

Your emotions can be similar in that some things you can see why they have set you back, and you can fix them easily, but there will also be bigger problems where you need outside help. Don't spend your life in the darkness when someone can help. You may need to see different people to help with different problems, but don't give up until the lights come on again and you find yourself buzzing with energy, smiling and laughing with joy.

EXERCISE 37:

Think about how Energy can help or hinder you. Using H.E.L.P.S. in the previous chapter and list one example of each:

	Root Cause	Key
H	_____	_____
E	_____	_____
L	_____	_____
P	_____	_____
S	_____	_____

....

Positive Energy is Attracted to Positive Energy.

....

Your energy is like a magnet with two poles that pull and push. Think about how your energy affects the people around you, and think how their energy affects you.

Setting Energy Goals

Think about setting yourself a goal involving energy, no matter how big or small make it relevant to your circumstances and skills around energy. This may be your own energy level or learning to wire your own radio or something different around energy.

What is the goal you want to set?

_____

_____

_____

What is your current status?

_____

_____

_____

What steps do you need to take in between?

_____

_____

_____

If necessary, write the steps out in a series of smaller steps, and break them down into as many smaller manageable steps as possible, on a separate piece of paper.

Parent Toolbox

Help your teenager by talking about all the positive energy they have held over the years, and how that made you feel. Tell them about the energy you experience that you want them to feel. Also listen to their energy level now, through what they say, think and do. Ask them how it makes them feel, and help them identify where this emotion fits with the HELPS and FLITE models of the book.

By now, the conversation should be enlightened and sought after, but life will be life, and this book will be the source of go-to help at any time when emotional energy is feeling low. I wish you all well and every success in reconnecting all your energies again as a family.

Key Points

I want to massively congratulate you for completing this book and taking incredible responsibility for your own emotional awareness and wellbeing.

My advice would be to keep this book somewhere safe and come back for inspiration any time you are feeling out of sorts. Simply using the structure of the book will help you dip in and out of the information to inspire your life to constantly fend off and negativity by creating change that matters.

FINAL NOTES:

Note any pages that really helped or any progress you want to
congratulate yourself on.

_____

_____

_____

_____

_____

_____

_____

_____

_____

_____

_____

_____

_____

_____

_____

_____

_____

_____

_____

_____

BRAIN UNCHAINED SUMMARY

1. **Next time you have that chained feeling of depression, feeling lost and suffering in darkness, remember how each part of this system helps break those chains...**

Now you have the Emotional Awareness to recognise your emotional state.

2. **With the emotional cycle, you have the power to STOP and THINK...**

Where do my emotions currently sit?

> Yellow – Happiness
> Red – Anger
> Blue - Sadness or
> Black - Depression

Where do I want my emotions to be?

Orange – Changes: Are you thinking positive or negative thoughts, or is the emotional change due to inner changes in your thinking, or outer changes in the world around you. Is it a combination of both?

3. **When you recognise that change of emotions, think about why it happened.**

What changed?

- Health
- Emotional
- Logical
- Physical
- Social

What are my Options?

When you know what changed, you may need to look at the keys to F.L.I.T.E. to discover the root cause first, then use your logic to work out which KEY solution fits with which H.E.L.P.S. option to provide you with your ideal options for positive change. What works for you may be different to someone else depending on your resources.

4. **When you know what changed - dig deeper and find that treasured Key.**

What was the root cause?

- Finance
- Links
- Information
- Time
- Energy

Which one is the Key to the options available to me?

Don't waste valuable energy on options that are not available. If all options are out of your reach or you have no access to any of the keys to flite, it's time to ask for help. That's your magic get-out-key when all else fails.

Remember that using this book over and over, and the exercises within, will lead to lifelong personal development, raise emotional awareness, create empathy, and lead to a happy and fulfilled life.

....

Mastering Life is all about Mastering change.

Kay Reeve

....

EMPATHY – PAYING IT FORWARD

Empathy is about taking all that understanding you have learned about your own emotions and starting to recognise the same emotional patterns in other people.

You can use your experience of overcoming emotional difficulties to support and guide friends, family, colleagues, and even your pets.

Look up 'Paying it Forward' as another personal development level where using empathy helps you support charities, create careers, enjoy greater friendships, learn leadership skills, and uses your emotional understanding to make the lives of those around you better, as well as taking care of your own emotions first.

I have enjoyed this journey of writing the book and hope you have learned a great deal from reading it.

If you have found this book super helpful, please let me know by leaving a review on Amazon, and better still, if you see a friend struggling with their emotional energy, tell them about the book too.

KAY AND HER SON MATTHEW

Depression is the loss of seeking happiness, and the cure to depression is to desire happiness.

Something was weighing me down, making me sad and resentful to the world and people around me. I didn't know what it was. When you don't want to get out of your cosy and warm bed in the morning, that is depression, except it's a bed of rusted nails in the open rain.

I had to find my wounds in order to heal them. Then I became whole.

My life of regret became our story of success.

Matthew Reeve

(A picture of Matthew's little girl – Kay's granddaughter)

AUTHOR AND TEDx SPEAKER

Kay has always had determination but never knew the power of it until she endured seeing her son go through the challenges of learning to live with Asperger's Syndrome, and dealing with suicidal depression.

It was through his journey that she discovered her emotional journey as a mum. She discovered emotions so powerful, she was driven and motivated to keep going no matter what happened. To give up on her son was as unthinkable as the consequences.

For many years, she just felt like she was keeping his head above water but didn't know how to get him onto safe ground. She was frightened for his life so many times and sad that he wasn't living his childhood to the full.

She had also spent seven years in active voluntary first-aid duty and learned there about taking care of your own emotions at the scene of an accident. She also studied basic counselling to help understand her son's depression and home educated him from the age of nine. At thirteen, he published his first 25,000-word novel called "The Red Dragon – A New Evolution". Now she was a proud mum.

In his later teens, he was suicidal again, and she was working as an administrator by now. She had some incredible management and leadership teams around her, who understood that much of her own anxiety was because she cared so much about her son. They also knew they could not help him, but they did help her. Tremendously!

The simple act of recommending personal development books, or taking just two minutes to talk to her, created a massive ripple effect. These books were aimed at people in business and careers, but she knew there were lessons in them that could help her son too. She studied and learned, sharing little nuggets with him along the way, but it wasn't working.

Then she realised it was because he needed something visual to learn from – and so Brain Unchained began. It was her experience of filing and sorting, organising and planning, as a career, that helped her apply the same processes with positive thinking, into organizing and explaining emotions.

During her years as an administrator and facilitator at the Offshore Windfarm, she also learned the skill of public speaking and took an adult education award, inducted new staff into the company, and delivered tool-box-talks to trade and service contractors. She was well aware of the importance of good communication.

This all helped her to write this book in some way – and keep paying it forward, in respect of those who paid it forward to help them.

*For more upcoming materials to support the book including **FREE printable worksheets** and online courses about the Mood Mentor Model, please visit www.kayreeve.co.uk*

*You can also find the TEDx Talk 'Tackling Teenage Depression' on YouTube by searching for **Kay Reeve***

Samaritan's number: Call any time 116 123
www.samaritans.org

ACKNOWLEDGEMENTS

Firstly, I would like to thank all the people who believed in me back in 2016 when the journey of this book began and to the FIVE incredible mentors who spent countless hours helping with my 2017 TEDx Talk. Also, to Sue Eastman for the belief she instilled in me to push boundaries and talk not just about what we had been through, but how I felt about it. She would ask - who is Kay?

Thank you to my parents for giving me a home again this summer when my world fell apart.

I would like to thank Dr David King for being a friend for *many* years online and teaching me to believe in myself. In his words, I would become a monster and not the green-eyed boggly kind.

Thank you to Nat and Jill for being an angel on my rock-bottom day. Tosin Ogunussi for being 'just there' when I needed this year, and powering me to achieve boundaries in record time – Done beats perfect, and it's not Impossible - I'm possible. Thank you.

Also thank you to Tosin for connecting me to agent Labosshy Mayooran of DVG Star Publishing, and to Labosshy for the instant connection we had over bringing this book to fruition in such a short timeframe. Well done, I loved working with you both and don't think this will be the end.

Thank you also to Rebecca Osborne for seeing the vision and creating it so beautifully on the cover. To Sophie and Kieron for helping me with last-minute branding and websites ready for the launch, and to many online friends and followers who lifted my spirits by following my live discussions online while I worked my way through writing the book during Lockdown2.

2020 ending on a high to help you discover a better future in 2021 and always.

TESTIMONIAL

I am grateful to be invited to write this book review, which I think is best introduced by the concept of change.

Change is the only constant thing in our lives that we can guarantee. I would like to view it as life's way of enriching our experiences because without it we wouldn't evolve as human beings.

As we grow older, we become more wiser to the way of life, but this book is geared for teenagers and young adults to navigate the terrains of our ever-changing lives.

Teenagers and young adults often are misunderstood, especially by their parents who can't fathom why their child is caught up in a cyclone of emotions whilst attempting to stay connected and grounded in a world that's constantly changing.

Kay's book, "Brain Unchained", where she explains about her Mood Mentor Model that offers teenagers and young adults a real lifeline by allowing them to express their emotions in a healthy way and acknowledging the root cause, so they are free to create a more compelling future for themselves.

This book, in my opinion, is a must-read for all teenagers, young adults and parents who have children within this age group. Superb effort Kay, in getting your book, "Brain Unchained" out in such a curious time for teenagers and young adults going through these uncertain times.

Your book represents an invaluable resource for teenagers and young adults to manage and fully understand their own emotions in order to navigate their own personal change safely.

Tosin Ogunnusi
UK Number 1 Empowerment Trainer
Author of, "Time To Break Free"

"Sometimes you just need a break in a beautiful place alone, to figure everything out."

Coco Chanel

Made in the USA
Monee, IL
07 November 2022

17299322R00144